Books and Islands in Ojibwe Country

Books and Islands in Ojibwe Country

Traveling Through the Land of My Ancestors

Louise Erdrich

HARPER ● PERENNIAL

NEW YORK ● LONDON ● TORONTO ● SYDNEY ● NEW DELHI ● AUCKLAND

HARPER ● PERENNIAL

A hardcover edition of this book was published in 2003
by the National Geographic Society.

BOOKS AND ISLANDS IN OJIBWE COUNTRY. Copyright © 2003, 2014 by Louise
Erdrich. All rights reserved. Printed in the United States of America. No part of
this book may be used or reproduced in any manner whatsoever without written
permission except in the case of brief quotations embodied in critical articles and
reviews. For information, address HarperCollins Publishers, 195 Broadway, New
York, NY 10007.

HarperCollins books may be purchased for educational, business,
or sales promotional use. For information please e-mail the
Special Markets Department at SPsales@harpercollins.com.

Map © 2003 by the National Geographic Society.
Drawings © 2003 by Louise Erdrich.

FIRST HARPER PERENNIAL EDITION PUBLISHED 2014.

Designed by Michael Ian Kaye and Tuan Ching,
Ogilvy & Mather, Brand Integration Group

Library of Congress Cataloging-in-Publication Data

Erdrich, Louise.
Books and islands in Ojibwe country : traveling through
the land of my ancestors / Louise Erdrich.
pages cm
"A hardcover edition of this book was published in 2003 by the
National Geographic Society"—Title page verso.
Summary: "An account of Louise Erdrich's trip through the lakes and islands
of southern Ontario with her 18-month-old baby and the baby's father,
an Ojibwe spiritual leader and guide"—Provided by publisher.
ISBN 978-0-06-230996-9 (paperback)
1. Ojibwa Indians—Lake of the Woods Region. 2. Erdrich, Louise—
Travel—Lake of the Woods Region. 3. Erdrich, Louise—Family.
4. Lake of the Woods—Description and travel. 5. Lake of the Woods
Region—Description and travel. 6. Islands—Lake of the Woods
Region. 7. Lake of the Woods Region—Social life and customs. I. Title.
E99.C6E63 2014
971.3—dc23   2013048438

HB 07.15.2024

for Nenaa'ikiizhikok and her brothers and sisters

Contents

Books and Islands in Ojibwe Country

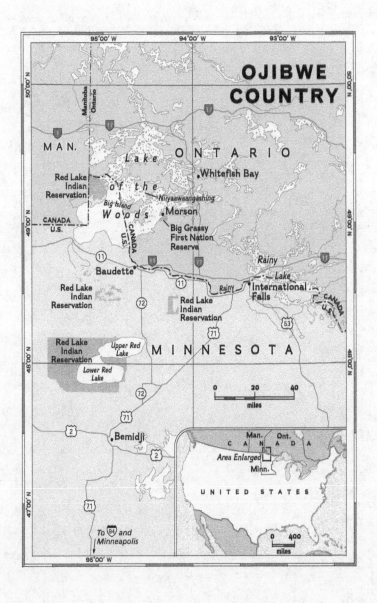

1

Books and Islands

My travels have become so focused on books and islands that the two have merged for me. Books, islands. Islands, books. Lake of the Woods in Ontario and Minnesota has 14,000 islands. Some of them are painted islands, the rocks bearing signs ranging from a few hundred to more than a thousand years old. So these islands, which I'm longing to read, are books in themselves. And then there is a special island on Rainy Lake that is home to thousands of rare books ranging from crumbling copies of Erasmus in the French and Heloise's letters to Abelard dated MDCCXXIII, to first editions of Mark Twain (signed) to a magnificent collection of ethnographic works on the Ojibwe that might help explain the book-islands of Lake of the Woods.

I am not traveling alone. First my eighteen-month-old and still nursing daughter and I will pop over the Canada-U.S. border and visit Lake of the Woods and the lands of her namesake, her grandmother. Then we'll dip below the border and travel east to Rainy Lake. We'll put about a thousand miles on our car and several hundred on other people's boats. I'm forty-eight years old and I can't travel aimlessly. I always seem to have a question that I would like to answer. Increasingly, too, it is the same question. It is the question that has defined my life, the question that has saved my life, and the question that most recently has resulted in the questionable enterprise of starting a bookstore. The question is: Books. Why? The islands are really incidental. I'm not much in favor of them. I grew up

on the Great Plains. I'm a dry-land-for-hundreds-of-miles person, but I've gotten mixed up with people who live on lakes. And then these islands have begun to haunt me, especially the one with all of the books.

Mazina'iganan is the word for "books" in Ojibwemowin or Anishinaabemowin, and *mazinapikiniganan* is the word for "rock paintings." Ojibwemowin is the Algonquin language originally spoken by the Ojibwe people living throughout Michigan, Minnesota, Ontario, Manitoba, and on into North Dakota. As you can see, both words begin with "mazin." It is the root for dozens of words all concerned with made images and with the substances upon which the images are put, mainly paper or screens. As the Ojibwe people began to watch television and go to movies, the word came in handy. *Mazinaatesewigamig.* Movie Theater. *Mazinaatesijigan.* Television set. They had a root word ready to make into a verb way back when Edward Curtis and later Ernest Oberholtzer came to photograph them. *Mazinaakizo.* To be photographed. (Nothing about stealing souls in the word mazinaakizo. Photographers did not take Ojibwe souls, it wasn't that easy. Soul theft required the systematic hard work of inventive humiliations and abuse by the government and by Catholic nuns and priests.)

The Ojibwe had been using the word *mazinibaganjigan* for years to describe dental pictographs made on birchbark, perhaps the first books made in North America. Yes, I figure books have been written around here ever since someone had the idea of biting or even writing on birchbark with a sharpened stick. Books are nothing all that new. People have probably been writing books in North America since at least 2000 B.C. Or painting islands. You could think of the lakes as libraries. 2000 B.C. is only the date of the oldest archaeological evidence found in the area we are going to visit. Traditional Anishinaabe people find the land-bridge theory a concept convenient to non-Indians and insist they've been here forever. And in truth, since the writing or drawings that those ancient people left still makes sense to people living in Lake of the Woods today, one must conclude that they weren't the ancestors of the modern Ojibwe. They were and are the modern Ojibwe.

Books. Why?

Because our brains hurt.

How a Mother Packs

For a week before I leave on any trip, I am distracted and full of cares. Just at the last minute, I always find myself doing things that I have put off for months, even years. I always change my will, then clean out cabinets and file old letters. I make certain that we all have sufficient underwear, that money and phone numbers are in relevant hands, the dog's vaccinated for Lyme disease, the manuscript of the last book is in production, the baby has her shots. Then I get more specific to the trip itself. I read books on pictographs and decide which notebooks to take along. Change the oil in the car. Make sure that my older daughters have postcards and shampoo. I buy tobacco—not to smoke but to offer to the spirits of the lake and the spirits of the rock paintings we will visit. I gather gifts for the paintings—a ribbon shirt, some red cloth, sage bundles. I purchase 124 disposable diapers and one of those baby harnesses I see mothers using in malls. If the baby goes over the edge of a boat or off an island, I picture myself hauling her right up. I go over plans for house-sitting and financial reports and make certain that our bookstore doesn't need me. There are so many small things. It is the small things that will consume me. The sunblock. The elms that must be treated with fungicide. The shoes. The many sizes and types of shoes girls wear all through their lives. I tell myself that God and meaning are in the small things as well as in the vast. But where in the wilderness of shoes is God? In the laces? The rubber bumpers? The heels that swiftly rise at age twelve?

On the other hand, none of this matters at all. The attention to details is just a way to stave off facing the truth. I hate leaving home.

Home

My 103-year-old house is surrounded by great trees. I have named each one of them. There is Guarding Elm that leans and tosses to the west, just beyond the blue gate. Tiny Offshoot of the Great Wahpeton Maple grows alongside, only six feet tall. It is still shaped like a drumstick. I grew it from a seedling that took root in one of my mother's flowerpots. Awkward and Shy are the elms that flank these two trees and Old Stalwart, biggest tree in the neighborhood, stands guard around the corner, in front of the house. Pensive Lover and Serene Darling, Haywire and Entire Trust are the locust trees that have sprung up in a ragged line along the edge of the yard. I have great admiration for these trees as they seem unkillable and their fronds of tossing leaves provide an ever shifting and trembling pattern of shadows on the old cream-colored walls inside our house. Also, they leaf out last of all and lose their leaves last, too, every fall, providing one final bank of burnished glory before the blastoff into winter.

Our house was built as a wedding gift for a father's much-adored daughter. His house, same layout, still stands next door. This house was built when the lake to our east was still a marsh, before it was dredged. Our house even looks a bit like a wedding cake, trimmed with spindle rails, bows carved over the window, egg and dart molding, and a couple of round peephole windows. Perhaps one day we'll attach a cheesy fifteen-foot plastic bride and groom to the roof. During the sixties, our house was gutted and became a rooming house, then a duplex. The interior lost its charming details and became just peculiar. Guests have seen a ghost on the top floor and the girls hear it walking. They believe he is a confused man, and that's what we call him. Sometimes, when one of my older daughters is gone for a while, the baby and I will sleep in her room so that the ghost of The Confused Man does not take up residence. I describe all of this because there can be no traveling unless there is a leave-taking. And the traveling is all the more in earnest if the leaving is difficult. For me, leaving hurts. This is the dwelling of four essential beings. My daughters. Even when they are not here, all of their things are here. We don't mean to become attached to things, but we do and rather than live in complete clutter, we are always culling, throwing, giving.

We have a lot of books in our house. They are our primary decorative motif—books in piles on the coffee table, framed book covers, books sorted into stacks on every available surface, and of course books on shelves along most walls. Besides the visible books, there are the boxes waiting in the wings, the basement books, the garage books, the storage locker books. They are a sort of insulation, soundproofing some walls. They function as furniture, they prop up sagging fixtures and disguised by quilts function as tables. The quantities and types of books are fluid, arriving like hysterical cousins in overnight shipping envelopes only to languish near the overflowing mail bench. Advance Reading Copies collect at bedside, to be dutifully examined—to ignore them and read Henry James or Barbara Pym instead becomes a guilty pleasure. I can't imagine home without an overflow of books. The point of books is to have way too many but to always feel you never have enough, or the right one at the right moment, but then sometimes to find you'd longed to fall asleep reading *The Aspern Papers*, and there it is.

Books. Another reason. I can take home along anywhere in the person of a book, and I do. I pack W. G. Sebald's *Austerlitz*. I bring Jim Crace's *Quarantine* and *Being Dead*. Then I add *Saints and Strangers* by Angela Carter, and *The Stone Diaries* by Carol Shields, which everybody else has read. That takes care of fiction. As for nonfiction, I never go anywhere without *A Concise Dictionary of Minnesota Ojibwe*, John D. Nichols and Earl Nyholm. I take along Joe Paddock's book on Ernest Oberholtzer, *Keeper of the Wild*. And then I pack a bag containing all of my baby's books, many of which I've laboriously blotted with Wite-Out, removing the English, and replaced with Ojibwe words written in Magic Marker.

Ojibwe

Ojibwe is also slurred into the word Chippewa and in its original form, Anishinaabe, it is pronounced Ah-NISH-in-AH-bay. The word is very loaded and bears a host of meanings and interpretations and theories. I've heard that Ojibwe refers to the puckering of the seams of traditional moccasins, or *makazinan*. Or that the Ojibwe roasted their enemies "until they puckered up." Gruesome. I've heard that Anishinaabe means "from whence is lowered the male of the species," but I don't like that one very much. And then there is the more mystical Spontaneous Beings. The meaning that I like best of course is Ojibwe from the verb *Ozhibii'ige*, which is "to write." Ojibwe people were great writers from way back and synthesized the oral and written tradition by keeping mnemonic scrolls of inscribed birchbark. The first paper, the first books.

The Blue Minivan

I am connected to and believe in my 1995 blue Windstar Minivan. We have history. I know exactly how to pack this vehicle, and feel its personality is with me as I fill the crevices between, under, behind the blue cloth seats. The blue Windstar is sisterly, accommodating, personable. And a gallant hauler. Used to be, I'd pack six preteen girls, two dogs (large Aussies), and myself in along with a week of food, clothes, games, and drawing materials, for a trip to a whole other island in Lake Superior where I did research while the girls swam, screamed, ate, screamed, roasted marshmallows, screamed, read "Wonder Woman" and "Catwoman" comics, slept, screamed, and woke, screaming happily, for a week or two. I don't really know how I have accomplished anything, ever. The minivan has been to North Dakota many times to visit Wahpeton, where my parents live, and to South Dakota, bearing my favorite sun dancer, my baby's father. With the backseats removed, he could sleep comfortably on a futon. The Windstar came back a little bloodstained, loaded with slabs of pipestone, great barrel-sized bundles of sage, a small prayer flag tied to its antenna. It made a traveling home for the sun dancer, the man whom we'll soon meet, who was named after low-lying clouds over the water of the lake we are going to visit.

Nenaa'ikiizhikok

This is what I have been told. There are four spirit women who take care of all of the waters of the world. One woman cares for the oceans of salt water. A second woman cares for the freshwater lakes, streams, and rivers. Yet a third woman cares for the waters inside of women that surround and cushion their babies. The fourth woman looks after the rains, the clouds, the storms, the waters in the sky. That woman cleans the sky up after a thunderstorm, makes sure the clouds are moving. The stars properly fixed in their places. She's always hard at work healing and arranging the sky so that things flow in the right order and direction. The baby in the car seat directly behind me is named for that spirit woman, Nenaa'ikiizhikok. Her grandmother on her father's side had this name, and was called Kiizhikok, Sky Woman, or Kiizhik; Sky, for short.

The original Nenaa'ikiizhikok was an imposing woman, tall and strikingly intelligent. The only image I have of her is from the back row of a boarding school class picture. She's blurred, of course, but obviously beautiful—not pretty—her features are too strong and cunning for merely pretty. This Nenaa'ikiizhikok is spoken of in Ojibwemowin as Nenaa'ikiizhikokiban. The "iban" at the end puts her in the past, in the spirit world, where I imagine she is still dancing in her jingle dress. She was a well-known expert jingle-dress dancer, and even came to the Turtle Mountains to powwow. My mother, Rita Gourneau Erdrich, grew up in the Turtle Mountains. My family is still there so I visit as often as I can. I like to imagine Nenaa'ikiizhikokiban dancing with one of my mother's aunts, maybe Jane or Shyoosh.

Baby Nenaa'ikiizhikok also has my mother's name, Rita. So she's a grandmotherly little baby, I guess. She even has one gray hair growing on the back of her head. I'm old to be a new mother of course, and so's her dad. Our baby was born a great-aunt. But we won't get into that. As my brother Ralph says, a look of distress on his face, "Don't say anymore about it! I knew she'd be something like a *great-aunt* already! I just don't want to know!"

Right now Kiizhikok is playing with her baby cell phone.

The plastic cell phone keeps saying "yellow triangle." It is a teaching cell phone. She drops it and picks up her teaching hammer. It says, "Can we fix it? Yes, we can!" She drops it, and picks up a musical box that lights up and plays bits of Mozart and Bach. She drops that and picks up a bright baby tape recorder that plays her late great-uncle Kwekwekibiness singing the Lake of the Woods song, which was given to the people in dreams by the lake itself. Eventually, she turns that off. Eats a cracker. As befits a child born with a gray hair, she is a very philosophical baby, personable and good-natured. She fusses for perhaps five minutes. Sleeps for two hours as we travel along a highway that was expanded from a road that was once a trail, an old Ojibwe trade route, heading north.

Songs traveled this route, and ceremonies, as well as pelts and guns. Medicines, knowledge, sacred shells, and secular ideas traveled this road, but never at sixty-five miles per hour. The van is kind, the van is good. She's got new brake pads and an alignment. She'll get us there.

Asema, Age, and Gratitude

The word for "tobacco" is *asema,* and it is essential to bring some for this reason: Spirits like tobacco. Their fondness for the stuff is a given of Ojibwe life. Tobacco offerings are made before every important request, to spirits or to other humans. Tobacco is put down by the root if you pick a plant, in the water when you visit a lake, by the side of the road when starting a journey. Tobacco is handed to anyone with whom you wish to speak in a serious manner. It is given for a story, or as an invitation to join someone in a teaching or writing project. Tobacco begins every noteworthy enterprise and is given as a thank-you at the end of every significant event. Perhaps spirits like tobacco because they like the fragrance of its smoke, or because people like tobacco and they appreciate thoughtfulness.

My grandfather made the old-time *kinnickinnick,* red willow tobacco, a smoking mixture of shaved willow bark, sage, and other local herbs. Ojibwe people still use and make red willow tobacco, but the tobacco offered these days is most often bought in pipe shops or purchased in small foil packets. Sometimes I'm offered cigarettes to help with projects or to listen to someone's problem. I quit smoking years

ago. I began to cut down once I started running, for I soon
realized that rolling a Bull Durham ciggie after a painful
three-mile jog and puffing away to recover was counterpro-
ductive. So as I am now pure, I dismantle the cigarette,
place the tobacco on the ground, then either bury or throw
away the filter. My favorite tobacco comes from a pipe shop
in Minneapolis and is called Nokomis, the Ojibwe word for
grandmother. It is a rich, black, softly shredded moist stuff

with a darkly sweet scent. Before I take a trip like the one I
am taking now, I always buy a pound or two of this tobacco
and divide it into smaller bags. Some are for the baby to give
to other people, and some are for the spirits of the places
we're going to visit.

There was a time when I wondered—do I really believe
all of this? I'm half German. Rational! Does this make any
sense? After a while such questions stopped mattering. Believing or not believing, it was all the same. I found myself
compelled to behave toward the world as if it contained sen-
tient spiritual beings. The question whether or not they *actually* existed became irrelevant. After I'd stopped thinking
about it for a while, the ritual of offering tobacco became
comforting and then necessary. Whenever I offered tobacco

I was for that moment fully there, fully thinking, willing to address the mystery.

Therefore, I've taught my children to offer tobacco (at the same time that I rail at them not to smoke it). The baby is adept at dipping her hand into the bag and waiting for the right moment to scatter the flakes. If allowed to, she'll keep offering tobacco until the bag's used up. She does it with such a sweet solemnity it's hard to stop her. *N'dawnis*, my daughter. I still am amazed to find her here.

Actually, I put down a *lot* of tobacco when I found out that I was going to have a baby. I needed every bit of spiritual help I could get. Maybe I'll get used to the fact that she is here by the time I'm sixty-four years old and clapping wildly at her high school graduation. When I walked into my midwife's office with a positive pregnancy test, one of my first questions was, "What kind of statistics are there on women who have babies at forty-seven?" Gently, I was told that statistics were unavailable because "there just aren't that many women having babies at forty-seven."

Still, I was dazzled. I felt like Mary at the Annunciation. Mary with PMS. I wept, I snarled, I laughed like a hyena. I knew that I was frightening to others, filled with a bewildering array of hormones. I'd gone from perimenopausal to violently pregnant. On the wall behind my midwife there was a framed poster of that obnoxious poem about the woman who looks forward to getting old so that she can wear purple. I happened to be wearing purple that day, and I was old, and I was pregnant. What did this mean? Along with the dazzled feeling I was struck by the awful burden of it all. How would I do it? I don't suppose the Virgin Mary felt sorry for herself, but I did. Then suddenly, I thought of a most wonderful consolation.

Books. Why?

To read and read while nursing a baby.

2

Islands

The Problem of Meeting Up
in Ojibwe Country

By the end of the first day we are in Bemidji, Minnesota, home of giant replicas of Babe the Blue Ox, Paul Bunyan, and, most importantly, where my brothers live now. Louis Erdrich, named for my German grandfather, is an environmental engineer who oversees all of the systems managers throughout the northern tier of Ojibwe country down here in the United States. He is in charge of making sure that reservations all through Michigan, Wisconsin, and Minnesota have adequate water and sewage and waste disposal systems. This is a vast job, but Louis deals unflappably with toxic waste and buried gas tanks. My other brother, Ralph Erdrich, Jr., is the head emergency room nurse at Red Lake Hospital on Red Lake Reservation, just north of Bemidji. He sews up local brawlers, delivers babies, and extracts quantities of fishhooks from various parts of Red Lake Ojibwe bodies. We

have some difficulty deciding where to meet for dinner, at
Perkins or Country Kitchen. As we all worked at a Country
Kitchen in Wahpeton, North Dakota, me as a waitress and
hostess, and my brothers as cooks, there is a nostalgia factor.
But as, therefore, we also know exactly what went on behind
the scenes at Country Kitchen, we opt for Perkins.

The interior is crowded, steamy, loud with families.
Between the two of them, my brothers have five sons and
one tiny new daughter. We're sitting around three pushed-
together tables, ordering baskets of onion rings and hash
browns and chili and sandwiches, when I am suddenly over-
come by a great feeling of happiness. My brothers are loyal
and kind fellows, and they have seen me through tough
times. When my husband died in 1997 they took off work to
come and stay with me, to answer the telephone and guard
my children. They also made sure I didn't stay in bed all day,
or chew the woodwork. They helped the household keep on
functioning. They kept my world partly normal. They are
tall and sturdy and they make me feel safe. Now, as we sit
in Perkins eating deep-fried foods and dressing-drenched
salads, I am again comforted by their solid presence. We
don't have to be analytical, we don't have to be literary, we
don't have to talk about anything at all, really. It is enough
to be together to enjoy the continuity and the weird Erdrich
history.

They are tireless professionals in their work, but sweet
and nonjudgmental in their personal lives. They are what
women in the Midwest call "guy guys." They do guy things
like fish and watch football, refurnish furniture, and tinker
with dangerous electrical wiring. In their guyness they relate

easily to my guy, Tobasonakwut, the sun dancer and the father of Kiizhikok. They ask about him and about my plans for this trip. I am forced to say that, as usual, I have no exact idea how I'll actually meet up with him. Although, as always, I am sure it will happen.

Meeting up is always complicated in Ojibwe country, and never seems to happen as it was planned. Tobason-akwut, who is a traditional healer, as well as a tribal politi-cian, teacher, and negotiator, is always being called on life or death missions. He has devoted his life to helping people. He is a one-man spiritual ER. And so, when making plans, I have found it best to be prepared to wait. I have found it best to understand things will always change and take a long time. Important and essential items will be lost, mis-laid, then found, and then they will need to be repaired. I have found it best to travel with everything I need in order to spend a comfortable night, anywhere, even in my car. I spend one, though at Bemidji's Holiday Inn Express. The next morning, as soon as Kiizhikok and I have investigated the "continental breakfast" and partaken of four kinds of dried cereal, including Froot Loops, we drive straight north past Red Lake Reservation on US 72, heading for Baudette, where I'll cross the border.

I'm revved up on a cup of unfamiliar coffee. Holiday Inn Express coffee. Kiizhikok drifts off after operating a plastic blender that chimes "Old MacDonald" in the barks of dogs, the croaks of frogs, or the mews of cats, or all at once. This strangely complicated toy was made in China. I am very happy as I now get to glimpse some of my favorite country. The great *mashkiig*, or bog, between Red Lake and Lake of the Woods, is traditionally the great Ojibwe pharmacy. It is full of medicines. There is Labrador tea, or swamp tea, *makigobug*. Snakeroot, which I should be carrying for good luck and health on this journey. There is balsam, a laxative. *Ininiwunj*, or milkweed, used on whistles as a charm for drawing deer. Pitcher plant or *omukikiwidasun*, which makes great toys. The Ojibwe name means "frog leggings." There is willow for indigestion, for basketmaking, the inner bark for kinnickinnick and headaches. *Makibug*, sumac, for dysentery. White cedar for coughs. Highbush cranberry, blueberries, Juneberries, wild currants, gooseberries. *Winabojobikuk*, for snakebite. That's "Winabojo's arrow." *Winabojo nokomis winizisun*, painted cup, or "Winabojo's grandmother's hair," used for rheumatism and for the diseases of women.

One medicine I do use is a *ginebig*, or snake medicine. I've got some in a plastic baggy. Puffball powder is the spores of dried puffballs, collected from those white, round, low-growing mushrooms that grow everywhere, even on city boulevards. Put this powder on a cut or a scrape and it heals immediately. All of these medicines and countless others grow on either side of the highway in the tamarack bog, an ecosystem so vibrantly rich that traditional Ojibwe teachers and healers still go out to fast there, to show their respect for the medicines and to learn from these plants.

Red willow, stands of maple, watery alder, and birch give way at last to neat little towns and isolated farms. Up near the border, at Baudette, we buy supplies and also phone cards. The phone cards are often useless in Canada, but I buy them anyway. And then we are across the border and heading up to Morson, Ontario, through Big Grassy First

Nation Reserve on a familiar little highway dotted with construction crews repairing the constant erosion and washouts. I park the blue minivan at a dock in Morson. The owner of New Moon fishing lodge, Rocky Moen, helps me unload the van and transfers the duffels, the camera equipment, the portable crib, into the lodge boat.

Rocky is a kindly and intelligent man and seems devoted to the ecology of the lake. We start talking immediately about the rock paintings as we proceed directly to the island that his family has owned since the 1950s. Rocky is intrigued with the paintings near his lodge, and he is still angry about the defacement of those paintings decades ago. "Stupid, stupid, stupid," he says. "It bothers me a lot. I know the person who did it." When I ask the person's name, though, Rocky just looks pained. The trip to the island takes about forty-five minutes, and as the mainland is blazing hot this July the cool breeze is a relief. Kiizhikok stands in the whipping wind, and I hold tightly onto the handle on the back of her life jacket and grasp one leg, too, just to make sure.

Boats make me very uncomfortable. At any moment, I think we'll ram into a rock. The boat will sink. But I'll still be gripping the baby. I'll tow her to shore. There are plenty of islands around here, and I never go out onto the lake without carrying in my pocket a Ziploc baggy of waterproof matches. Once I tow the baby to shore, I'll light a fire, fan the smoke, and eventually someone will come to investigate. We will be saved. During this short ride, I become so lost in my fantasy of boat wreck that it is only with a wrench that I return to the immediate fact that we are traveling along, so far so good, and we're not capsizing. Rocky seems completely at home on the lake. We'll probably be safe. I don't relax my grip on Kiizhikok, but I do force myself to abandon my fantasy and look around at the stunning beauty.

The islands jut from the lake, tall with hundred-year pines, rocky and severe. The water glitters with power and great tangles of second-growth bush ride by, cut with sloughs and passageways. High cliff faces shadowed with caves loom over us and there are dense island groupings, great lazy white rocks sprawled like animals just above the water. Clusters of birds, pelicans, appear to stand right on the water but are actually balancing on the tips of dangerous underwater reefs. Once I'm lost in the actual beauty of the lake, I relax a little and it isn't long before we are drawing up to the lodge dock where a young Ojibwe man named Riel—for Louis Riel, the great French-Ojibwe Métis leader who came near to establishing a Métis Nation—helps us disembark.

KIIZHIKOK AND I settle ourselves into a cabin with a window that catches breezes off the lake. We'll hear loons laughing madly all night, sometimes close and sometimes echoing from shore to shore. Outside, the great rock we're staying on slopes dramatically into deep water. My baby actually *could* fall off this island. Still, living here will make it easy to set up our trips out to see the rock paintings. In the past, we've camped out on the islands, deciding from day to day where to pitch a tent. But I don't want to camp with baby along. She's quick, she's curious, she's smart, and she likes to put rocks in her mouth. Maybe when she's older we can deal with open fires, slippery reefs, bugs, poison ivy, and wood ticks. Well, the wood ticks we'll deal with anyway. Here's one. Here's another. They're inevitable up here. Right now, Kiizhikok appreciates a bit of grass to run across and a predictable routine.

A period of emptiness, unusual to my life, now begins, in which I can either fret or accomplish that rare thing, *the doing of nothing*. Or rather, with the baby, *the doing of what the baby wants*. This kind of doing is very much part of the trip, and although there is a dreamy blankness to it—the hours merge and the edges of the days grow fuzzy—these times when I devote my whole self to Kiizhikok are also times of great complexity and learning.

I learn, for instance, that she can keep a little stone in her mouth for an entire day. The second morning on the island I see her bend over, pick up a little white oval stone, and touch her mouth with it. But when I pry her mouth open, I can't find it. Perhaps I've just imagined that it went in. She gives me a betrayed look, clenches her jaws, and so I quit searching for the rock. We eat our breakfast and then we put on swimming suits. We sit for hours on one side of the island watching crayfish, *ashaageshiinhyag*, as they emerge in spidery shadows from the cracks of a half-submerged rock. They are fearless and dart for our toes, waving pincers. We remove them with sticks so we can ease off the rock and bob around in the lake together in our bright red life jackets.

We surprise an otter who has come to feast on the ashaageshiinhyag. He circles a cabin with a sinuous lope and then in confusion starts toward us. He pauses on the clipped grass of the island lawn. A huge glossy boy, his whiskers quiver comically as he takes our measure. With a fabulous flop he is down the rock, in the water, paddling off on his back. He watches us for a long time before he ducks under and is gone.

I'm very happy now. I wanted to see an otter on this trip because they are among my favorite animals and we know their feasting ground, just ten miles north. This place is in Seamo Bay. There, Kiizhikok's grandmother and namesake, the original Nenaa'ikiizhikok, played as a child. The otter's picnic ground is a large rock where we always find empty turtle shells. It is rather sad, but I can't help thinking how conveniently packaged a turtle is to an otter. Like a kind of Big Mac in a crushproof box. When visiting the otters' lunch spot, scattered with perfect empty shells, it is impossible not to imagine the otters lolling around sucking the turtles out and maybe munching a side of lichen or crayfish.

Late that night, as I am getting little Kiizhikok ready for bed, I see an unfamiliar flash of white and fish the stone from her mouth. I hold it in my hand and look at her in distress. My sister and brother-in-law are pediatricians. This stone is a classic choking hazard. Do you understand that, Kiizhikok? Choking hazard? I look into her warm round face and try to explain. She puts her hand on my arm in a motherly way and shakes her head indulgently. I recognize the look. My teenage daughters give it to me. *Oh, Mom, I'm fine and you just worry too much.* My head whirls. *Yes, everybody else was drunk and high on crack and heroin and many other drugs you haven't heard of don't want to and worst of all they were keeping stones in their mouths, choking hazards, while having unprotected sex, so I sat outside the party on the porch with the fireflies and thought about how I don't need to do these things to have a good time.*

I'm getting anxious about my daughters.

The fact that they are utterly responsible and I know they are safe doesn't matter. I have *got* to worry.

I'm also getting anxious about Tobasonakwut.

All of this time, Tobasonakwut is trying very hard to get to us. I always know that. I imagine that he must find a way to tow his boat to the lake, and then to dry out some spark plugs in the motor, probably. As well, he will encounter various other delays, all based on quirks of the boat and requests from other people. Besides, it is summer and that is the busiest time for Ojibwe people.

For the past two months, Tobasonakwut has been helping people meet their spirits. He does this by putting them out to fast for visions. He puts people in his sweat lodge, then into his boat, drives them out to an island, leaves them there for four days, worries and prays for and checks on them during those four days, then picks them up and feeds them ceremonially and assists them in understanding their experience. He has put out hundreds of people and picked them up hundreds of times and listened to their dreams and helped them understand their insights and their suffering. When he picks them up, as they have not eaten or drunk water during those four days, as they have heard or seen things unexpected, as they have been alone in the night and often frightened, they can barely speak. They have a certain look in their eyes. He is very careful with them.

He has been very careful with the three people, friends, who arrive the next day. I'm very glad. Now I have people

to wait for him along with me. These people have fasted at
the pictographs that we will visit. Every time they come to
Lake of the Woods, they come prepared to become extremely
hungry. This time they have decided to experience the lake
in a new way—full. On the way here, however, they couldn't
help stocking up on food and drink. They have developed
a Pavlovian response to the lake and find it hard to believe
that they will be fed. But they are fed, and copiously. The
food at the fishing lodge, provided by a dedicated cook named
Donna, is right out of small-town North Dakota—it is haute
cuisine if you lived in Wahpeton during the mid-'70s. A relish
plate. Prime rib, thick cuts of ham, tiny bowls of cauliflower
drenched in cheese sauce, always some form of potato—
mashed, fried, scalloped—and pitchers of iced tea. Homemade
bread. Baked chicken. Pie. Salads of iceberg lettuce and pale
tomato. Kiizhikok sits high on her booster seat and eats with
a fork. (She's talented at this. We think it betokens an unusual
and preternaturally advanced hand-eye coordination. Perhaps
she'll be a famous baseball player. I won't allow her to become
a fighter pilot.) Her red napkin is tucked around her neck. All
around us great stuffed fish leap and gape on the walls. I feel
increasingly like one of them.

The Lake, or Tobasonakwut, or Tobasonakwut, the Lake

Tobasonakwut arrives. During the last fifteen minutes of
northern dusk light he pulls up to the dock. There he is,
looming toward us with fixed weariness. I have just decided

that he and the lake are one person. That is a relief. For if to describe one is also to describe the other, I am set free. Both are so vast and contradictory and full of secrets that I both despaired of and was delighted with the prospect of never getting an adequate handle on them. But now that he has actually arrived, I feel that I should introduce Tobasonakwut.

To do so, I must go back to 1688 when a twenty-year-old French explorer named Jacques de Noyon wrote about a group of people who nearly killed him when he raided their gardens of squash, corn, pumpkins, beans, and potatoes on what is now Garden Island in Lake of the Woods. According to Tobasonakwut, as de Noyon and his men approached the gardens, an arrow was fired from the woods and landed at their feet. As any rational people would, they stopped, and then from those trees there emerged a giant people, taller than any native people they'd ever met, and very frightening. He got to know them a little, and called them the People of the Cat.

Those people were Tobasonakwut's ancestors, who became the Big George family and are of the Bizhiw or Lynx dodem. Tobasonakwut's people still tend to be tall, rawboned, rangy (handsome, I think), and with a wariness that can shift from kind to belligerent. They are not a people to be trifled with. But for all that, Tobasonakwut is exceedingly gentle. Babies seem to know this. Around my extended family, he's always the one who sits and talks to the babies. Yet he's tough in a way people who have been through too much are tough—he can sleep anywhere. Or go for days without really sleeping when his presence is required in ceremonies. Yet although he went hungry as a child, he

won't eat just anything. He's finicky about his food now.
He doesn't eat much meat, passes on frybread, orders salads
in restaurants—unusual eating habits for an Ojibwe. As I
said, he's full of contradictions, like the lake. Tobasonakwut
grew up on a spit of land called Niiyaawaangashing, in a
time before the Ojibwe or Anishinaabeg were removed from
their homes in the islands. He is fortunate to know something of the time when his community was intact, when
the bays were dotted with cabins and camps, when his extended family lived more or less by the spiritual seasons of
the *Midewiwin*, the Grand Medicine teachings, and those
ceremonial teachings formed the moral and social center of
the community. The teachings made sense of the beauties
and hardships of Ojibwe existence. He was also unfortunate,
for that world was thrown asunder in just a few years. After
his people had stabilized their lives and partly recovered
from the wave of nineteenth-century invasions and diseases,
the Canadian government invented devastating aboriginal
policies. It is his burden to have seen what survived of the
Ojibwe world around him nearly demolished by death, re-
moval, forced relocation, the poison of alcohol, and to have
experienced an education that amounted to kidnapping and
a brutal attempt at brainwashing.

The place where Tobasonakwut grew up, Niiyaawaangashing, is about three or four miles by water from the fishing
lodge. It is very useful for us to have a base of operations so
close to the places we want to visit, but it is not uncomplicated.
Camp owners have become almost the only residents in land
that once belonged, and by treaty rights should still belong,
solely to the Ojibwe. The only native people staying at the

lodge now are the fishing guides, Riel, and two other men. Tobasonakwut once worked as a fishing guide. But he knows and is part of the lake in a much more profound way than where to catch walleyes for wealthy non-Indian sport fishers. He knows the lake in a way that only indigenous people can truly know anywhere.

At one time, everyone who lived near the lake was essentially made of the lake. As the people lived off fish, animals, the lake's water and water plants for medicine, they were literally cell by cell composed of the lake and the lake's islands. Tobasonakwut's father once said to him, *The creator is the lake and we are the waves on the lake.* Tobasonakwut shows us the place in the heavens from which the creator descended. Their origins are familiar. The cosmology is in the surrounding landscape, in the stars, in the shapes of the rocks and islands, and in the mazinapikiniganan, the paintings that his people made on the sides of the rocks.

Niiyaawaangashing

The next day, we get into a sixteen-foot Alumacraft with a 115-horsepower motor, and we buzz out onto the lake. Before anything else, we go to visit Niiyaawaangashing. There are still two fish-camp houses standing and one tumbled-in cabin of weathered wood. Two docks twisted and upended by ice. A strong little black bear stands next to the first dock, watching us calmly. We cut the motor. The bear slides into the channel and dog-paddles with powerful assurance to the other side, where he doesn't hide himself at all, but stands up and rakes the berry bushes underneath a tree containing a huge eagle's nest. One eagle hulks stubbornly next to the nest, watching over an eaglet, whose head pops up, curious, from time to time. We skirt a long, pale boulder with a crease down the middle, just opposite the former camp, romantically secluded.

"Hundreds of Anishinaabeg were conceived on that rock," says Tobasonakwut. I look at the gray hollow in the rock—it actually looks pretty comfortable. Nobody lives at Niiyaawaangashing anymore, except the bears and eagles, and so we stop only long enough to put down tobacco. Sometimes the bears, especially the curious young, sit in the trees and watch people on the shore. Sometimes a little bear will get caught in the crotch of a tree and hang himself. When such a skeleton is found, it is very sacred to the Ojibwe and is used in religious ceremonies. Once when Tobasonakwut was little, there was a big Midewiwin or Grand Medicine lodge in the grass that is now quickly returning to scrub trees and sumac. A Midewiwin lodge is made of young bent-over popple or birch poles tied together with basswood. Spruce boughs or ferns are tied along the sides for shade. The main events of the religion are carried out in the lodge. When Tobasonakwut was about six years old, a strange event took place at the Mide lodge here at Niiyaawaangashing.

Tobasonakwut's Memory

He watched six canoes approaching from the west, one bearing a man and dog. They pulled to shore, and the explanation for their coming was given. The man with the dog had suffered an oppressive dream. It was a dream he could not mentally evade even once he woke. In the dream, he'd learned that he once had been a slave owned by the Bwaanag, who were for generations bitter enemies of the Ojibwe. As a slave, this man dreamed that he had been tied up with the dogs and, like the dogs, fed scraps, not fed at all, despised and kicked and beaten. One afternoon he just was about to die of sorrow and loneliness when it occurred to him to speak to the dog next to him, who answered. The dog told him that the dog people had been waiting for the man to talk to them. Now that he had spoken, they were willing to help him escape the Bwaanag.

There will be some feathers, said the dog, and you will chase them. When the Bwaanag look at you, they will not see a man. They will see a dog playing with some feathers. You will run after the feathers until you are far from the Bwaanag camp.

In this way, the man was freed from his degradation. The man who dreamed he was the man enslaved by the Sioux understood when he woke that he and his dog must give thanks to those dream dogs by fasting together. And so the canoes had come, accompanying him to the Midewiwin lodge, where he would fast for twelve days, his dog for four days. During those twelve days, the children were to treat the man just as the Bwaanag had, mean. Though they were to respect the dog. Tobasonakwut could not be cruel to the man, who cried and groaned in his hunger, as he lay in the lodge. The dog fasted alongside his master, and then was feasted like a human being. The man continued until he weakened so badly he could not move. But he survived, and in the end he was feasted too.

There is nothing where that lodge was but poison ivy and grass and a broken table. Tobasonakwut's dream is to rebuild the lodge there and to teach people all that he knows, including what the rock paintings mean. To this end, he has started a foundation to gather money to put up this lodge. He has also filed a claim for compensation against the Oblate Order of the Catholic Church. They were in charge of his education, but instead they stole life, innocence, and spirit from him and from his people. He thinks they should be responsible for helping to reconstruct what was lost.

Perhaps someday a Mide lodge will stand where the table has collapsed. Perhaps the old Midewiwin songs will be heard on Niiyaawaangashing once again.

Nagamonan

Songs belong to these islands. When Ojibwe people fast in these islands, the songs, even if lost for a time, always come back in dreams. The *nagamonan*. These very old songs are as old as the rock paintings. Songs were composed, often by those who owned drums, for honor, for celebration, for beauty, for love. There is one particular song that haunts Tobasonakwut and has, as well, a special meaning for me. Our friends often sing this song in their sweat lodge. It is a song used to help those struggling with the pitiless, uncanny, and baffling disease that is alcoholism. The words of the song, *Kiiwashkwebiishki indigo anishaa dash indigo*, are the words of a long-ago drunk who found his way to sobriety not through a twelve-step program, but through the intervention of a powerful spirit. All of this happened during the eighteenth century, when the fur trade began the first wave of alterations that would forever shift the economic, social, and spiritual balance of Ojibwe life in Lake of the Woods.

Tobasonakwut always begins his story of this song by attributing it to his uncle Kwekwekibiness. Very traditional people are very careful about attribution. When a story begins there is a prefacing history of that story's origin that is as complicated as the Modern Language Association guidelines to form in footnotes.

In this story, there was a young man, an extraordinary hunter, known as unusually strong and of a generous nature. He began to sell his furs to the first trader in the islands. At first, the young hunter acquired blankets, fire strikers, kettles, guns, and ammunition. He traded for things he needed, his family needed, his wife, his children. But eventually, he traded for liquor too.

A form of trader's rum, mixed with hot pepper and tobacco, became his pleasure. He bought a little more each time he came with piles of beaver skins. The trader began to provide him with the liquor before they finished their negotiations, and soon the young man woke from long binges and found that he owed the trader, that he had drunk up his pay and then some. At last, he began trading for the rum alone. His children left him, his wife left him, his whole family stayed away from him. The animals stayed away from him too. It was no use hunting, so he traded his gun for a keg. It was no use trapping, so he drank away his traps. Finally, it was no use begging either. No use in anything. The trader's liquor had eaten his life, his loves, his strength, his mind, his will, and all but a fraction of his spirit.

This tiny part of his spirit, this fraction of the man that was still a man, decided that it would disappear into the wilderness. So the young man walked away from the trading house and from all of the trade goods including the rum. He walked off into the snow without a blanket and without a gun. He walked until he was blinded by the snow glare, exhausted to the last degree. In the deepest moment of despair he'd ever known, he threw himself down in a trackless place, at the mercy of the spirits. While he was face down in the snow, and as he determined that he surely would die, he heard a song.

The nagamon began like this, Kiiwashkwe biishki indigo anishaa dash indigo. I am a drunk. I am nothing. The song went on and he sang the whole of it into the place beyond the bottom of a drinking cup that is the darkest place on Earth. As he sang this song, over and over, and as he waited to die, this young man heard a voice.

It was the voice of the Kwiingwa'aage.

The Kwiingwa'aage is a spirit of dark strength and cleverness represented by an animal, the wolverine. Among the Ojibwe, this animal has an almost supernatural reputation. There is one who steals from your traps and cannot be caught. There is one who you know is watching you, but you cannot see him or hear him. There is an animal who follows you just out of sight. It is deathless, lonely, and somewhat strange in his contempt for human intelligence.

He easily outwits the smartest hunters. When the creator passed near the Earth in the form of a tailed light, that was the Kwiingwa'aage. When a man feels eyes at his back and experiences a thrill of unreasonable fear out in the woods, that is the Kwiingwa'aage. Perhaps because he is so fearless, so impervious to pain, so dangerously strong, the spirit of the Kwiingwa'aage is the only one that can address the problems of the *schkwebii*, the alcoholic. For the disease is without pity just as is the animal. Alcohol is cunning, and it is phenomenally deceptive. So when the animal spoke to the young man, and said that he had been watching him, and that he had given this young man a song, it might have been the first time the Kwiingwa'aage was known to pity anyone.

And if it was the first time that this spirit had showed pity, in all the years of Ojibwe hardship, then it goes to show how terrible this scourge of alcohol was, and how low it laid the people.

The voice of the Kwiingwa'aage saved the young man though, and he got rid of the trader's poison and recovered his life.

There are no Anishinaabeg, including mixed-bloods like me, whose lives have not been affected by the perplexing pains of addiction. The degraded longing and despair of alcoholism changes even the most intelligent among us. And so when we regard the place where the song given by the Kwiingwa'aage was first heard by the young man so long ago, it is for me a personal moment. I hold our baby tighter and we put out handfuls of tobacco.

The Four Stones

Tobasonakwut's copy of the big book of Alcoholics Anonymous is covered with a handmade leather case. It is marked and thumbed, interleaved with personal notes and ribbons. It is like a preacher's bible, or a writer's favorite dictionary. He has carried the twelve steps with him for over thirty-five years, but his uncle, Kwekwekibiness, who knew nothing of the steps, surprised him once by telling him something about the book that he had not perceived.

Kwekwekibiness was devoted to the sweat lodge ceremony, in which stones are super heated and then cooled with water to produce a healing steam. In every Ojibwe ceremony, the number four is sacred—four seasons, four directions, four phases of life, four of everything. Kwekwekibiness held Tobasonakwut's book and told him that it contained four stones. Intrigued, Tobasonakwut examined the book for the stones and after reading it painstakingly found three. He couldn't find the last until one day he noticed, in the beginning of the book, a gravestone.

John Tanner and the Landscape of Hunger

This is John Tanner country—where he was always hungry. One of my favorite books, *The Falcon, a Narrative of the Captivity and Adventures of John Tanner During Thirty Years Residence among the Indians in the Interior of North America*, is about the relentless efforts of a man to feed himself. My sisters and I read this book in its old Ross and Haines edition until the spine gave, the pages tumbled out and were held together with a rubber band. John Tanner's narrative exerted a fascination on us, and not only because one of our ancestors was mentioned in its pages, but because of the enigma of John Tanner himself. My sister Lise says that it is the only true sequel to that great American novel, *The Adventures of Huckleberry Finn,* which ends when Huck and Jim light out for the territory. On the first page of his narrative John Tanner wishes, as a boy, that he could go and live with the Indians. During the next few pages he is, indeed, captured by the Shawnee. It is 1789, and the rest of the novel is about what exactly happens in the "territory."

John Tanner was brought north, sold, adopted, and from then on lived entirely as an Ojibwe. For the most part, he hunted throughout Lake of the Woods country and into Rainy Lake, the exact range of the area I'm visiting on this trip. I've read his narrative so often that it is a constant mental reference. I see this region as it is and was. When I think about John Tanner's life the flimsy billboards, border crossings, cheap plastic gas station signs, and hopeful fishing lodge ads look pathetically superimposed on a region harsh, mystical, quite beyond the practical efforts of human beings to tame it. Out here on the lake, those human efforts are sparse and seasonal. It doesn't take much imagination to see myself in Tanner's world.

John Tanner led a feast or famine life. His tale was told after he had attempted to return to civilization and found its restrictions irksome. Tanner, whose Indian name was Shawshaw-wa-Be-na-se, or Falcon, was captured at nine years old, specifically to comfort a woman who'd lost her own son. But his stepfather and brother nearly killed him and he was fortunate enough to be sold to an extraordinary and resourceful Ojibwe woman, Net-no-kwa, whom he came to love. His portrait of Net-no-kwa is a treasure. Tanner had a gift for description and an ear for anecdote, and in his voice Net-no-kwa is a stereotype-busting powermonger. When she approached the fort at Mackinac with her flag flying from her boat (it was probably a flag that described her personal dream vision), she was saluted by the fort's gun. She was a shrewd trader, an observant hunter, and a medicine woman who also got smashed on whiskey from time to time. She saved her family many times with her resourcefulness in times of crisis, and she and Tanner developed a particular affection for one another. "Though Net-no-kwa was now decrepit and infirm," he says near the end of her life, "I felt the strongest regard for her and continued to do so while she lived."

Tanner had a clear eye and in his narrative he provides detailed descriptions of the world around him. A terrified female bear picks up her cub and cradles it like a human. He recounts his surprise at a porcupine's trusting stupidity and notes that it was quite tasty. An otter exhausts him with its tenacious fury when he tries to kill it with his bare hands. Tanner attended to animal behavior with a terrible fixity of purpose, for game was the only real food and his relationship with nature was one of practical survival.

At the leanest times, Tanner's family was forced to boil and eat their own moccasins, to subsist on the inner bark of trees or dead vines. During the best of times, the food was eaten all at once and drink, if there was any, consumed until it disappeared. Indeed, the kind of life where a few people killed a fat moose and polished it entirely off in a few days is mirrored in the binge or abstinence style of drinking that Tanner describes. Not a life for the moderate. Not a life for the faint of heart. Tanner's ordinary feats of hunting endurance are almost beyond comprehension in these days of radio-collared bear dogs and high-powered telescopic rifles. And yet he was by his own account no more than a mediocre hunter, who was patiently instructed by Ojibwe who had survived for millennia without guns or steel:

> I had occasion to go to the trading house on Red River, and I started in company with a half-breed . . . who was mounted on a fleet horse. The distance we had to travel has since been called, by the English settlers, seventy miles. We rode and went on foot by turns, and the one who was on foot kept hold of the horse's tail and ran. We passed over the whole distance in one day.
>
> When I returned to my family I had but seven bullets left, but as there was no trader near, I could not at present get more. With those seven I killed twenty moose and elk. Often times, in shooting a moose or elk, the ball does not pass entirely through and can be used again.

Visiting his family in Kentucky after having lived virtually all of his life in the north woods, John Tanner fell ill. He grew claustrophobic when nursed inside of a house, and had to sleep outside in his brother's yard to restore his strength.

Once he returned to Sault Ste. Marie and told his story, he vanished. He was suspected of a murder but that charge was later thought false. He never turned up. As Lise says, "He vanished into his own legend." His end was as mysterious and tragic as the outline of his life in this beautiful, unforgiving country. As he was to all respects a "white Indian," and saw the world as an Ojibwe, his is the first narrative of native life from an Ojibwe point of view.

3

Rock Paintings

One of the first questions people ask about the rock paintings is how old they are—complicated answer. There is no completely accurate way to date rock paintings. Some are hundreds of years old, and others thousands of years. The Anishinaabe have been in Lake of the Woods forever, according to Tobasonakwut. Since at least two thousand years before the birth of Christ, according to archaeologists. One thing certain is that the paintings were made by the ancestors of the present-day Anishinaabeg, for the ancient symbols on the rocks are as familiar and recognizable to Tobasonakwut as are, say, highway and airport and deer crossing signs to contemporary Americans. Of course, the rock paintings are not just pointer signs. They hold far more significance. They refer to a spiritual geography, and are meant to provide teaching and dream guides to generations of Anishinaabeg.

Akawe Asema

The rock paintings are alive. This is more important than anything else that I can say about them. As if to prove this point, we see as we approach Painted Rock Island that a boat has paused. It is a silver fishing boat with a medium horse-power outboard motor. A man leans over and scoops a hand-ful of tobacco from a pouch, places it before the painting, and then maneuvers his boat out and goes on. *Akawe asema*. First offer tobacco. This makes Tobasonakwut extremely happy, as do all the offerings that we will see as we visit the other paintings. It is evidence to him that the spiritual life of his people is in the process of recovery. He swerves the boat out and chases down the man who made the offering, and then, seeing who he is, waves and cuts away. He is doubly pleased because he knows where this man sets his nets, and knows that he went ten or twelve miles out of his way to visit the rock painting. It is sunset now and will be dark before the man returns to his dock.

The Wild Rice Spirit

The long rays of the deepening sun reach through the chan-nel. As we draw our boat up to the rock painting, the light warms the face of what was once a cliff. I am standing before the rock wall of Painted Rock Island and trying to read it like a book. I don't know the language, though. The painting spreads across a ten- or twelve-foot rectangle of smooth rock, and includes several spirit figures as well as diagrams of teachings. The deep light pulls the figures from the rock. They seem to glow from the inside, a vibrant golden red. For a long while, I am only interested in the visual experience of standing at eye level with the central figures in the rock. They are simple and extremely powerful. One is a horned human figure and the other a stylized spirit figure who Tobasonakwut calls, lovingly, the *Manoominikeshii*, or the wild rice spirit.

Once you know what it is, the wild rice spirit looks exactly like itself. A spiritualized wild rice plant. Beautifully drawn, economically imagined. I have no doubt that this figure appeared to the painter in a dream, for I have had such dreams, and I have heard such dreams described. The spirits of things have a certain look to them, a family resemblance. This particular spirit of the wild rice crop is invoked and fussed over, worried over, just as the plants are checked throughout the summer for signs of ripening.

This year, on Lake of the Woods, the rice looks dismal. Because the high waters have invaded a whole new level of recently established rice beds, the rice is leggy and will flop over before it can be harvested. Earlier in the day, we stopped to examine Tobasonakwut's family rice beds. At this time of the year, mid-July, the rice is especially beautiful. It is in the floating leaf stage and makes a pattern on the water like bright green floating hair. *Kiimaagoogan*, it is called. But upon pulling up a stalk Tobasonakwut says sadly, "There's nothing in this loonshit," meaning he cannot find the seed in the roots. All the energy of the plant has gone into growing itself high enough to survive the depth of the water. There will not be enough reserve strength left in the plant to produce a harvest. "And then," Tobasonakwut goes on, "if your parents had no children, you can't have children." In other words, the rice crop will be affected for years.

So perhaps this year it is especially important to ask for some help from the Manoominikeshii.

When the pictures were painted, the lake was a full nine feet lower, and as it is nearly four feet higher this year than usual, some paintings of course are submerged. The water level is a political as well as natural process—it is in most large lakes now. From the beginning, that the provincial government allowed the lake levels to rise infuriated the Anishinaabeg, as the water ruined thousands of acres of wild rice beds. As it is, I mentally add about one story of rock to the painting, which at present lies only a few feet out of the water.

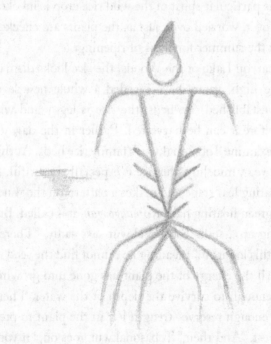

This is a feminine-looking drawing. The language of the wild rice harvest is intensely erotic and often comically sexualized. If the stalk is floppy, it is a poor erection. Too wet, it is a penis soaking in its favorite place. Half hard, full, hairy, the metaphors go on and on. Everything is sexual, the way of the world is to be sexual, and it is good (although often ridiculous). The great teacher of the Anishinaabeg, whose intellectual prints are also on this rock, was a being called Nanabozho, or Winabojo. He was wise, he was clever, he was a sexual idiot, a glutton, full of miscalculations and bravado. He gave medicines to the Ojibwe, one of the primary being laughter.

The Horned Man

This is the figure that glows brightest from the rock. He is not a devil, and he isn't throwing away a Christian cross—the local white Christian interpretation of the painting, which has led to its close call at defacement. (At the figure's far right, in white paint, I can still make out Jesus Christ in fairly neat lettering. But the thirty-year-old graffiti has nearly flaked off, while the original painted figures still blaze true.) As I stand before the painting, I come to believe that the horned figure is a self-portrait of the artist.

Books. Why? So we can talk to you even though we are dead. Here we are, the writer and I, regarding each other.

Horns connote intellectual and spiritual activity—important to us both and used on many of the rock paintings all across the Canadian Shield. The cross that the figure is holding over the rectangular water drum probably signifies the degree that the painter had reached in the hierarchy of knowledge that composes the formal structure of the Ojibwe religion, the Midewiwin. The cross is the sign of the fourth degree, and as well, there are four Mide squares stacked at the figure's left-hand side, again revealing the position of the painter in the Mide lodge.

I quickly grow fond of this squat, rosy, hieratic figure. His stance is both proud and somewhat comical, the bent legs strong and stocky. His arms are raised but he doesn't seem to be praying as much as dancing, ready to spring into the air, off the rock. When this rock was painted on a cliff, the water below was not a channel but a small lake that probably flooded periodically, allowing fish to exit and enter. Per-

haps it was a camping or a teaching place, or possibly even a productive wild rice bed. Very likely it was a place where the Mide lodge was built, like Niiyaawaangashing. The painter may have been a Mide teacher, eager to leave instructions and to tell people about the activities that took place here.

Most of the major forms of communication with the spirit world are visible in this painting—the Mide lodge, the sweat lodge or *madoodiswan*, the shake tent. The horned figure beats a water drum. Such drums are extremely resonant, and their tone changes beautifully according to the level of the water and the player's skill at shifting the water in the drum while beating it. (Anyone curious about the sound of the water drum can buy a CD and listen to the winners of a recent Native American Grammy, the singers Verdell Primeaux and Johnny Mike, *Bless The People*.) The water drum is a healing drum. In the pictograph a bear floats over the drum, and a line between the horned figure and the bear connects them with the sky world.

The line is a sign of power and communication. It is sound, speech, song. The lines drawn between things in Ojibwe pictographs are extremely important, for they express relationships, usually between a human and a supernatural being. Wavy lines are most impressive, for they signify direct visionary information, talk from spirit to spirit. In the work of some contemporary Ojibwe artists, Joe Geshick, Blake Debassige, and of course Norval Morrisseau, the line is still used to signify spiritual interaction. Contemporary native art is not just influenced by the conventions invented by the rock painters, it is a continuation, evidence of the vitality of Ojibwe art.

The Bay of Baby Spirits

Looking on a map at the little bay we are going to travel, my friend, who is in training as a *doulah* or birth assistant, says no wonder it is known as the home of baby spirits—the bay is thin and winding and looks like a fallopian tube. The bay of little spirits is a courting bay, the water shallow and romantic. To either side, the rich young undergrowth is said to be inhabited by the spirits of babies who choose humans, as they pass, to come and live with. Traveling slowly down the shallow channel, I stroke the tender spot upon Kiizhikok's head, the fontanel, which has nearly shut. I've heard it said that until it does the baby still hears spirits talking. If they're out there, if they're talking to her, I hope they are warning her that it is dangerous to hide stones in her mouth.

Suddenly we come upon three young moose, gangly and playful. Instead of climbing onto land, one clomps into the water and then swims along beside us. Her long rabbity ears cock toward us from time to time, and she doesn't seem particularly frightened. Her Joe Camel nose held high, she rolls her eyes at us. Those odd Twiggy legs and knobby knees work smoothly, powerfully. A wonderful swimmer, she at last veers away into the reeds and cattails. I am very surprised that this happened. According to John Tanner the wary moose is the most difficult of animals to hunt. But then, these are very young moose and our baby is in the boat. I harbor the irrational notion that animals are curious about Kiizhikok and show themselves around her, that her presence is a kind of magnet to them. And it is true, not only do we see animals but they seem unafraid of her, like the otter, like the moose, and the constantly wheeling eagles and pelicans. The animals come close as if they want to get a good look at this child whose ancestors watched their ancestors, whose grandmother ate their grandmothers, whose father was stolen from among them by priests.

Mirage Islands

When the water is high like it is this year, large pieces of bog pull free of the lake bottom and drift all through the bays and channels. You fall asleep looking at a certain shoreline, memorizing the sweep of it, and by morning the shape has shifted and the bog has moved on. When these bogs attach to islands, they can change its shape instantly, but often they merely bounce against the island until they fall apart. Lodge owners get their guide boats out and push the bogs into the lake currents. Close up, rising out of deep water, they are deceptively solid looking. They are a rich biomass composed of reeds, young willow, *wiikenh*, cattails.

Cattails are a useful plant whose roots are edible, whose tails when puffed out are a perfect diapering material for the tender new bottoms of Anishinaabeg babies, used to stuff in the bags of cradleboards. Reeds were used for floor covering, woven into mats. Wiikenh, or sweetflag, is the star of the floating bog, though, a medicine with every possible use. "Where there is wiikenh, there are Anishinaabeg," says Tobasonakwut. Wiikenh is the ultimate medicine. He investigates each floating bog, hoping to pick it easily, for when rooted it is difficult to wrench from the mud.

Looking at these bogs it is easy to see how, once, when a raiding party of Bwaanag had camped in Ojibwe country, they were driven out by use of a floating bog. The warriors entered the bog from underneath and swam it to the shore of the Bwaanag camp, like Birnam Wood come to Dunsinane. From that bog, they attacked and drove the Bwaanag out.

Massacre Island

It is not considered wise to point a finger at any island, especially this one. The Ojibwe use mouth or head to indicate direction, and are often humorously mocked for "pointing with the lips." But it is impolite to point a finger at people, and the islands as well. Pointing at the islands is like challenging them. And you don't want to challenge anything this powerful.

Massacre Island is a forbidden place. Recently, two men who tried to fast there were bothered the entire night by ghosts. As we approach the island, I feel its brooding presence. I can't tell whether this island is a formidable place because of its history, or whether it possesses a somber gravity all on its own. But the very look of the place disturbs me. Massacre Island is located where the lake deepens. Sounds travel farther, the air thins, the waves go flat. Its rocks sloping down to the water are not the pale pink flecked granite of the other islands, but a heavy gray nearly black in places and streaked with a fierce red-gold lichen.

On this island, the Ojibwe wiped out an entire party

of Sioux, or Bwaanag. As Tobasonakwut tells it, the entire island was ringed by Ojibwe canoes. At a signal, the *zaasaakwe*, the war whoop, a terrifying and a bloodthirsty shrill, was raised. From one canoe to the next, it traveled, a ring of horrifying sound. The canoes advanced four times. The zaasaakwe was raised four times. On the last time, the Ojibwe paddlers surged all the way forward, beached their canoes, and stormed the Bwaanag. He shows where the warriors died, including one who staked himself into the earth and fought all comers who entered his circle, until he was overwhelmed.

Atisigan

The paint, *atisigan*, should be patented, says Tobasonakwut. It is an eternal paint. The Ojibwe Sharpee paint. It works on anything. When he was little he often watched the paint being prepared. It was used for other things, besides painting on rocks. For burial, for bringing people into the religion, for teachings, for decorating request sticks and Mide stakes.

The recipes for paints used by other tribes are often based on vermillion from outcroppings of cinnabar. The Inuit used blood and charcoal. Burnt plum seeds and bull rushes were mixed into a black paint by the Klamath, and many tribes used blue carbonate of copper. Later, as we walk the Kaawiikwethawangag, the Eternal Sands, I will find some of the mysterious ingredients of the Ojibwe atisigan at my feet, then jumping from the lake.

Obabikon

On a great gray sweep of boulder, high above Obabikon channel, a rock painting gives instructions to the spirit on how to travel from this life into the next life. Such a journey takes four days and is filled with difficulties. For that reason, loved ones provide the spirit with food, spirit dishes, and encouragement in the form of prayers and songs. We climb to the painting with tobacco and leave handfuls by the first painting, a line with four straight, sweeping branches, and the second painting, which is of a *mikinaak*, or turtle.

The mikinaak has immense significance in Ojibwe life. As there are thirteen plates in its back, it is associated with the thirteen moons in the yearly cycle, and also with women. It was women, says Tobasonakwut, who were responsible for beginning Ojibwe mathematical calculations. They began because they had to be concerned with their own cycles, had to count the days so that they would know when they would be fertile. They had to keep close track of the moon, and had to relate it to their bodies in order to predict the births of their children. And they had to be accurate, so that they could adequately prepare. In a harsh Ojibwe winter, giving birth in an unprotected spot could be lethal. Women had to prepare to be near relatives and other knowledgeable women. Mathematics wasn't abstract. It was intimate. Dividing and multiplying and factoring were concerns of the body, and of survival.

Whitefish Bay

To get into Whitefish Bay from where we are will require lots of sandwiches, water, a full gas tank, and two extra five-gallon plastic gas containers that ride in front when full. We start early on a tremendously hot morning. By now, I'm much happier in a boat. I still have the usual fantasy, on starting out, involving the rock and the swim to shore towing Kiizhikok, but by now I'm used to it. I try to move on quickly and enjoy the breeze whipping with heroic fresh-ness off the lake. Whitefish Bay connects to Lake of the Woods via a peculiar contraption called a boat trolley. This is a suspicious-looking, wood-ribbed basket that the boat is floated onto. By sheer muscle power, turning a big red metal wheel that moves the trolley basket along a set of metal tracks, the boat is painfully transferred. Once on the other side of the concrete channel, we reload ourselves and start off, into Whitefish Bay.

First, we pause at the place where Tobasonakwut was born, a quiet little bay of old-growth pine and soft duff. Just after he and his brother were born, Tobasonakwut's name was discovered by his father, who gazed out into the bay and saw a certain type of cloud cover, low and even. Tobasonakwut. His twin was named for a small bird that visited his mother shortly after the birth. She has told Tobasonakwut that as this is the type of bird who nests in the same place year after year, if he ever sees one on a visit it will be a relative of the one who named his brother.

As he is sitting beneath a tree that must have been a sapling when he was born, as he is singing to his daughter, I realize that after thousands of years of continual habitation and birth on the shores of this lake, Tobasonakwut is one of the last human beings who will ever be born out on these islands.

Wiikenh

Wiikenh tea strengthens the immune system. Mixed with a mashed waterlily root, *okundamoh*, it draws out infection and poison. Speakers chew wiikenh to keep their throats clear, and singers chew it to strengthen their voices at the drum. As we enter a long channel filled with shallow water and small flooded bays, Tobasonakwut sees vast clumps of bright green-gold reeds and mutters, over and over, "So much wiikenh!" This is not the gloating sound I've heard before in his voice when discovering so much medicine. Rather, he is distressed that it should be sprouting in such tremendous abundance and no one else has come to pick it. His tone implies that this should all have been harvested, that the endless thick fringe of plants along the shores is an almost painful sight. One thing is sure, he can't pass it up, and for about an hour we putter along, stopping from time to time for him to lean over the prow of the boat and pull up the long tough bundles of muddy roots. He slices them off with a very sharp hunting knife while I sit behind the wheel of the boat with the baby.

Wiikenh gathering is very boring to her, but she has decided to be lulled into a state of contemplation by a combination of breast milk and boat engine. Indeed, every time she gets into the boat now, she tips her head dreamily toward my nipple. I've grown used to having her there. I've filmed eagles and those young moose, dancing loons and *zhedeg*, pelicans, with one hand while she nurses away. Indeed, though I haven't mentioned it, I have been filming everything I've described all along, as well as somehow brandishing a pen and notebook, all while nursing. One grows used to it.

Sometimes I look at men, at the way most of them move so freely in the world, without a baby attached, and it seems to me very strange. Sometimes it is enviable. Mostly, it is not. For at night, as she curls up or sprawls next to me and as I fall asleep, I hold onto her foot. This is as much for my comfort as to make sure that she doesn't fall off the bed. As I'm drifting away, I feel sorry for anyone else who is not falling asleep this way, holding onto her baby's foot. The world is calm and clear. I wish for nothing. I am not nervous about the future. Her toes curl around my fingers. I could even stop writing books.

Spirit Bay

The name on the map is actually Devil's Bay, so tiresome and so insulting. Squaw Rock. Devil's This and Devil's That. Indian or Tomahawk Anything. There's no use railing. You know it as well as I do. Some day, when there is nothing more important to do, the Anishinaabeg will demand that all the names be changed. For it was obviously the rock painting at the entrance to the bay that inspired the name. It is not a devil, of course, but a spirit in communication with the unknowable. Another horned figure, only this time enormous, imposing, and much older than the one in Lake of the Woods.

This spirit figure, horns pointed, wavering, and with arms upraised, is fading to a yellow-gold stain in the rock. It is a huge figure, looming all the way up the nine- or ten-foot flat of the stone. At the base of this painting, there is a small ledge. Upon it, a white polo shirt has been carefully folded, an offering, as well as a pair of jeans. The offerings are made out of respect, for personal reasons, or to ask the spirit of the painting for help. There are three rolls of cloth, tied with ribbons. Asema. Again, here are the offerings, the signs that the rock paintings are alive and still respected by the Anishinaabeg.

Binessi

I get very excited when I see the thunderbird pictured on a cliff far above the water. It is so beautifully painted, so fluid and powerful even glimpsed from forty feet below. "Are you strong? Are you agile?" Tobasonakwut asks. "If you are you should climb up to that rock. You'll never be sorry that you did." I believe him. I grab my camera, my tobacco offering, and retie my running shoes. I already have my twenty extra pounds left over from having a baby. I am just pretending that I am strong and agile. Really, I'm soft and clumsy, but I want to see the painting. I am on fire to see it. I want to stand before that painting because I know that it is one of the most beautiful paintings I will have ever seen. Put up there out of reach or within difficult reach for that very reason. At that moment, I just want to see it because it is beautiful, not because I'll get some spiritual gift.

The climb is hard, though of course it looked easy from below. Like all women are accused of doing, I claw my way to the top. Sweaty, heart pounding, I finally know I'm there. All I have to do is inch forward and step around the edge of the cliff, but that's the thing. I have to step around one particular rock and it looks like there's nothing below it or on the other side. I could fall into the rocks. My children could be left motherless. Or I could simply get hurt, which is not simple at all. I calculate. The nearest hospital is hours away and there is that trolley contraption. So I don't go around the rock, but seek another route. I continue climbing until I'm over the top of the cliff. Still, I can't see down. I don't know how to get down to the paintings. Again, I nearly take the chance and lower myself over the cliff but I can't see how far I'd fall. Finally, looking far, far down at my baby in her tiny life jacket, I know I'm a mother and I just can't do it.

Climbing back into the boat is admitting defeat.

"Give me the camera, and tobacco," says Tobasonakwut.

"No!" I say. "Don't do it!"

"Why? If you can't make it then you'll feel bad if I do?"

"Just like a guy, so competitive! Because you *will* go around the corner of that rock and you'll fall and kill yourself."

"I will not fall. I've done this before."

"How many years ago?"

"A few."

With terse dignity, Tobasonakwut goes. He's an incredible climber and regularly shames the twenty-somethings who come to fast on the rock cliffs by climbing past them and even dragging up their gear. I know he'll make it. He'll do something ridiculous, maybe even get hurt, but he'll manage to get right next to the paintings.

He's always poking around in the islands. Once, he described a rockslide he started coming down from a cliff like this one. Remembering this, I maneuver the boat away from a skid of rocks on the south side of the cliff, though he didn't go up that route. Anyway, he had a terrifying ski down on the boulders and at the bottom one bounced high in the air, over him, and its point landed right between the first and second toe of his right foot. He said that he'd done something mildly offensive to the rocks. He'd thrown one down to see what happened. That's how the landslide started. When the boulder bounced down on his foot, he thought it would slice his foot off. But when he looked down his foot was still there. Just a crushed place between his toes. It was as if, he said, the rocks, the grandfathers had said, "Don't fool around with us."

And now he's climbing rocks again.

It's no use. The best I can do is make sure that the baby's comfortable. I might as well be comfortable too. I take a fat little peanut butter sandwich from the cooler and munch dreamily, while nursing, and after a while the wind in the pines and the chatter of birds lull us into a peaceful torpor. I forget to watch for him, forget the all important ascent. From somewhere, at some point, I hear him call but he doesn't sound in distress so I just let my mind float out onto the lake.

Then he's back.

"Did you see me up there?"

"No!" I feel guilty, awful. Here he is about as old as I'll be when Kiizhikok graduates from high school and I didn't take the trouble to film him as he made the dangerous climb to the rock paintings. He hands over the camera. Ashamed of my distracted laziness, I put it away.

"How did you do it?" I ask quietly.

"Oh, jumped."

"What?"

"Jumped."

I'm immediately just a little pissed off. "You jumped? You could have broken your leg!"

"It was only six feet."

"More like fifteen feet."

"Well, if you hang down, it comes to . . ."

"Don't ever do that again!"

We travel for a while, heading back for the boat trolley, and I brood on his unlikely stubborn-headed insistence that he's still a young man. How long will it take before he really hurts himself? He's scarred and burnt. Just last winter a red hot stone from a sweat lodge brushed up against his calf and left a deep hole. His back and chest are pitted with sundance scars and one of his eyebrows was smashed sideways in a boxing match. He took so many punches to the head while a boxer that he has to take special eyedrops now to relieve the pressure on his optic nerve.

"You've got to quit doing things like this," I say, but I know I will have no effect, and besides, this is one of the reasons I love him. He's a little crazy, in a good way, half teenager and half *akiwenzii*.

He doesn't answer, just keeps steering the boat, munching trail mix.

When we get to the boat trolley I am further convinced that animals love the baby because it happens again. This time it is a nice fat *waabooz*, a grown rabbit. The rabbit sees us from across the shallow boat channel and behaves just like a friendly little dog. It hops down onto the trolley mechanism while Tobasonakwut is laboriously turning the wheel. The little rabbit crosses the water using a rail as a bridge, and comes curiously up to me. The rabbit looks right at the baby. Just as when the otter came toward us, I'm a bit unnerved. I suddenly imagine that this rabbit will bounce charmingly close, and then bare vampire teeth. But it merely inspects us, turns, and hops away calmly.

All right, I think, animals *do* love the baby.

Now that we're over the channel and into Lake of the Woods again, I try hard to let go of my agitation about Tobasonakwut's dangerous rock climb. We start talking about the thunderbird pictured in the rock painting that I didn't get

to. I did take a movie picture of it and Tobasonakwut surely snapped some up-close shots, I think, consoling myself. That thunderbird is very graceful, and there is a handprint with it. It is still the most beautiful bird I have ever seen.

Binessiwag

These spirits are particular about what they're called— they prefer *Binessiwag* to *Animikiig*. They're very powerful. Thunder is the beating of their wings. Lightning flashes from their eyes. You don't want to rile the young ones, as they are the most unpredictable. When a storm approaches, traditional Ojibwe cover all the shiny objects—mirror and cooking pans—so as not to attract the attention of the binesiwag. A feather over the door lets them know Anishinaabeg are at home. They will avoid that house. It is important, when the binesiwag appear, at any time of the day or night, to offer tobacco.

The only natural enemy of these immensely strong beings are the great snakes, the *Ginebigoog*, who live underwater. These snakes are said to travel from lake to lake via an underground network of watery tunnels that lies beneath northern Minnesota and Ontario. There is an ongoing feud between these two powerful supernatural beings. The young binesiwag, those that come out in spring, are the most volatile. Anyone who has experienced a violent spring thunderstorm in the north woods can attest to this truth. But we have perfect weather. Day after day the morning sun shines clear. The Earth heats up. The water gleams like metal. The sky by noon is a hot deep blue.

The Eternal Sands

Kaawiikwethawangag, they are called, the Eternal Sands. John Tanner must have approached from the south, for he said, that "this lake is called by the Indians Pub-be-kwaw-waung-gaw Sau-gi-e-gun, 'the Lake of the Sand Hills.' Why it is called 'Lake of the Woods' by the whites, I cannot tell, as there is not much wood about it." And it is true, the lake is very different in character when approached from this direction. Gorgeous and deserted sand beaches stretch around the southeast side of Big Island, the reserve that Tobasonakwut's mother, the original Nenaa'ikiizhikok, came from. The great island is now empty of people, the villages abandoned since shortly after World War II.

Even though Canada's aboriginal people could not vote and were being forced from their lands and educated by force, they fought in both World Wars. One of Tobasonakwut's uncles, a soldier, came home to Big Island much affected by the fighting. He was silent, withdrawn, and stayed away from his family. Then his little son, a small boy named Wabijiis, came down with an unusual fever.

Such was the terror of disease, at the time, that it was decided that once the boy died the village would break up and the people disperse to Seamo Bay and Niiyaawaangashing. The little boy's grave was dug with paddles—the people wanted to bury him the old way and not use metal. A prayer flag was erected near. The little boy Wabijiis was the last person buried on Big Island, and his grave and all that remains of the village is now grown over with young trees.

Name (nam-ay)

All of a sudden between our boat and the fringed woods a great fish vaults up into the air. I've seen muskies. I walk around a Minneapolis lake of which signs warn MUSKELUNGE

ARE IN THESE WATERS. Once, I saw an Uptown Minneapolis type, dressed in tight black jeans and tight black T, wearing a suit jacket, fishing in a very cool way. Cool until he hooked a vast muskie. His screams echoed along the sedate bike paths and the fish he dragged forth was soon surrounded by Rollerbladers, joggers, and awestruck pink- and blue-haired teens. The fish I just saw was not a muskie. It was even bigger. Tobasonakwut sees it from the corner of his eye and slows the boat down.

"Asema," he says, and puts the tobacco in the water. That fish was the *name*. The sturgeon. Tobasonakwut is happy and moved to see it because, he says, "They rarely show themselves like that."

Once again, I'm sure it is the baby. The sturgeon seemed to take flight above the water, rising in a pale thrust and falling on its back. The sturgeon is a living relic of life before the age of the dinosaurs, and to see one is to obtain a glimpse of life 200 million years ago. I've never seen one of these fish in the wild before, much less grown large. I've only seen tiny Pallid Sturgeon. A relative of mine who works for the North Dakota Department of Natural Resources was raising sturgeon to stock the Missouri River. Name, *Acipenser fulvescens Rafinesque*, the Lake Sturgeon, is long-lived and can grow to more than eight feet. The Lake of the Woods record fish was a lake sturgeon weighing 238 pounds. Tobasonakwut says they can grow over twice that large. Males live into their forties. Female sturgeon can live over one hundred years, but they only spawn every four years, and not until they are in their twenties.

The sturgeon up here on Lake of the Woods were

the buffalo of the Ojibwe. Greed and overfishing by non-Indians caused their population to crash around the turn of the nineteenth century, when, along with the Great Lakes, Lake of the Woods became one of the world's principal suppliers of caviar. The sturgeon were indiscriminately taken by the non-Indian fisheries for their roe, much as the buffalo hunters took only the buffalo tongues. They were stacked like cordwood all along the lake and often left to rot. An agonizing sight for the Ojibwe, who revere the sturgeon and who knew its secrets.

Long before fish-farming, the Ojibwe had traditional "sturgeon gardens," shallow and protected parts of the lake where they mixed eggs and sperm and protected the baby sturgeon from predators. The eggs and sperm were mixed together with an eagle feather in an act both sacred and ordinary. These days, the Ontario Ministry of Natural Resources and tribal communities raise sturgeon. A conserva-

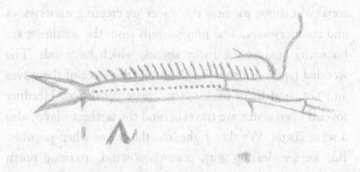

tion program begun ninety-nine years ago, in Lake Winnebago near Shawano, Wisconsin, has provided the best example and the best hope. Wisconsin has tightly restricted sturgeon fishing since 1903, and Lake Winnebago now has the only large, self-sustaining sturgeon population in the world. A long-term program there may provide stocks that will rehabilitate sturgeon in the Great Lakes and throughout Canada.

At the base of the very first rock painting that we visited, a great sturgeon floats above a tiny triangular tent. It is a divining tent, a place where Ojibwe people have always gone to learn the wishes of the spirits and to gain comfort from their teachings. Someday perhaps Kiizhikok's children will find the sturgeon vaulting from the water around Big Island a common sight. I hope so. It was a moment out of time.

Waves

On our way to visit the island and the Eternal Sands, we experience a confluence of shifting winds and waves. Tobasonakwut shows me how the waves are creating underwaves and counterwaves. The rough swells from the southeast are bouncing against the rocky shores, which he avoids. The wooded lands and shores will absorb the force of the waves and not send them back out to create confusion. Heading toward open water, we travel behind the farthest island, also a wave cutter. We slice right into the waves when possible. But we are dealing with yesterday's wind, a strong north wind, and swells underneath the waves now proceeding from the wind that shifted, fresh, to the south. I think of what Tobasonakwut's father said, "The creator is the lake and we are the waves on the lake." The image of complexity and shifting mutability of human nature is very clear today. Eventually, we beach our boat at the first little bay. Tobasonakwut starts out, at once, to comb for treasures.

I have the same feeling when I come upon a deserted beach as I do when entering a used bookstore with promisingly messy shelves bearing handwritten signs and directions, or a rummage sale run by beaming white-haired people who are handing out free coffee and look like they kept all of their forties soapbox glass dishes and their flowered tablecloths in the original plastic. As I look at the beach, strewn with driftwood and interesting rocks, I have the slightly guilty feeling that I get when I visit the gift shop before the museum. Sure enough, as baby and I beachcomb in the opposite direction from Tobasonakwut, we come across three magnificent eagle spikes, those feathers at the ends of wings, the ones used by sun dancers in their sage crowns. But the wind dies suddenly at the margin of the beach and we are edged from the fabulous pickings by biting blackflies and the big droning horseflies that drive moose insane. To avoid the flies, the baby and I take to water just like the moose do.

I plop down and let the waves crash into me at waist height while I nurse the baby. Occasionally her head is spritzed and refreshed. I am wearing a hat, lots of sunblock, dark glasses. The amber-colored water is too rough for leeches to grab onto my legs. I could sit here forever. The pelicans, zhedeg, pass over, twenty or thirty at a time, wheeling in strict formation when up high. Sometimes more casual, they sail down low and I see the boatlike prows of their breasts and drooping gullets. Crowds of black ducks veer over, too. There is a curtain of birds along this beach.

Rising and falling, the flocks constantly change and shift. Then, just before me, about seventy feet out, the great fish rears again. This time it hangs even longer in the air, catching sun on its belly, somehow joyous.

"It's all there," Tobasonakwut says upon returning, pointing behind me and then out to the open water.

"What?"

"Atisikan."

The paint that is eternal comes from the Eternal Sands. Just down the beach the waves have dragged the sand off the tough roots of a low beach plant. The roots are such a brilliant red that from a short distance it looks as though the leaves are bleeding into the water. This is a component of the sacred paint used in the rock paintings. And the fish who showed itself to me is a part of the atisigan too. Sturgeon's oil is one of the bonding agents that will not let go, one of the substances that makes the paint eternal.

Offering

I am almost asleep when I realize that I have seen all that is depicted in the first rock painting, the one that I marveled over, the one that glowed from the rock in all of its complexity. I saw the wild rice, which is the spirit of the wild rice, I saw the bear, I saw the deer, and I saw the name. The next morning, we go back to the painting. Tobasonakwut ties up at the base of the rock. I bring a dish of food, including asema, up to the top of the rock. I also leave my favorite ribbon shirt.

It is a leave-taking. I have to tell myself not to look back as we travel away from the rock. It is as though I've left behind something intangible—not the shirt, the tobacco, or the food. It is as though I've written a poem and burned it. Given up a piece of my own spirit. I don't understand the feeling that closes in on me. And even now, as I am writing in my study, and as I am looking at photographs I took of the paintings, I am afflicted with a confusing nostalgia. It is a place that has gripped me. I feel a growing love. Partly, it is that I know it through my baby and through her namesake, but I also had ancestors who lived here generations ago.

The Ojibwe side of my family, who ended up with the surname Gourneau, roamed from Madeline Island in Lake Superior, along what is now the Canadian border, through Lake of the Woods and down to Red Lake, and then out onto the Great Plains and eventually the Turtle Mountains. Baupayakiingikwe, Striped Earth Woman, was one of those ancestors, as was Kwasenchiwin, Acts Like A Boy. Our family was of the Ajijauk or Crane dodem, and the Makwa or Bear dodem. I can't help but imagine that these two women, whose names my mother and sister have searched out of old tribal histories, walked where I've walked, saw what I've seen, perhaps traced these rock paintings. Perhaps even painted them.

Ojibwemowin

My grandfather, Patrick Gourneau, was the last person in our family who spoke his native language, Ojibwemowin, with any fluency. When he went off into the Turtle Mountain woods to pray with his pipe, I stood apart at a short distance, listening and wondering. Growing up in an ordinary small North Dakota town, I thought Ojibwemowin was a language for prayers, like the solemn Latin sung at High Mass. I had no idea that most Ojibwe people on reserves in Canada, and many in Minnesota and Wisconsin, still spoke English as a second language, Ojibwemowin as their first. And then, while visiting Manitoulin Island, Ontario, I sat among a group of laughing elders who spoke only their own language. I went to a café where people around me spoke Ojibwemowin and stood in line at a bank surrounded by Ojibwe speakers. I was hooked, and had to know more. I wanted to get the jokes, to understand the prayers and the *aadizookaanag*, the sacred stories, and most of all, Ojibwe irony. As most speakers are now bilingual, the language is spiked with puns on both English and Ojibwemowin, most playing on the oddness of *gichi-mookomaan*, that is "big knife" or American, habits and behavior.

As I was living in New Hampshire at the time, my only recourse was to use a set of Ojibwe language tapes made by Basil Johnson, the distinguished Canadian Ojibwe writer. Unknown to Basil Johnson, he became my friend. His patient Anishinaabe voice reminded me of my grandfather's and of the kindest of elders. Basil and I conversed in the isolation of my car as I dropped off and picked up children, bought groceries, navigated tangled New England roads. I carried my tapes everywhere I went. The language bit deep into my heart, but I could only go so long talking with Basil on a tape. I longed for real community. At last, when I moved to Minnesota, I met fellow Ojibwe people who were embarked on what seems at times a quixotic enterprise—learning one of the toughest languages ever invented.

Ojibwemowin is, in fact, entered in the *Guinness Book of World Records* as one of the most difficult languages to learn. The great hurdle to learning resides in the manifold use of verbs—a stammer-inducing complex. Ojibwemowin is a language of action, which makes sense to me. The Ojibwe have never been all that materialistic, and from the beginning they were always on the move. How many things, nouns, could anyone carry around? Ojibwemowin is also a language of human relationships. Two-thirds of the words are verbs, and for *each verb*, there are countless forms. This sounds impossible, until you realize that the verb forms not only have to do with the relationships among the people conducting the action, but the precise way the action is conducted and even under what physical conditions. The blizzard of verb forms makes it an adaptive and powerfully precise language. There are lots of verbs for exactly how people shift position. *Miinoshin* describes how someone turns this way and that until ready to make a determined move, *iskwishin* how a person behaves when tired of one position and looking for one more comfortable. The best speakers are the most inventive, and come up with new words all of the time. *Mookegidaazo* describes the way a baby looks when outrage is building and coming to the surface where it will result in a thunderous squawl. There is a verb for the way a raven opens and shuts its claws in the cold and a verb for what would happen if a man fell off a motorcycle with a pipe in his mouth and drove the stem of it through the back of his head. There can be a verb for anything.

Tobasonakwut delights in the language, his first language. He loves to delineate the sources and origins of words, keeps lists of new words, and creates them himself. Yet, as with many of his generation, he endured tremendous punishment for this love. He remembers singing his father's song to comfort himself as he was driven to a residential school at age eleven. The priest who was driving stopped the car, made him get out, and savagely beat him. Tobasonakwut spoke no English when he first went to school and although he now speaks like an Ivy League professor if he wants to, he stubbornly kept his Ojibwemowin. Tobasonakwut says that the beatings and humiliations only made him the fiercer in loving and preserving his language. As he says this he clutches his heart, as if the language is lodged there. From the beginning, even as a child, he determined that he would speak it as often as he could.

For Tobasonakwut, Ojibwemowin is the primary language of philosophy, and also of emotions. Shades of feeling can be mixed like paints. *Kawiin gego omaa ayasinoon*, a phrase used when describing loneliness, carries the additional meaning of missing a part of one's own being. Ojibwe is especially good at describing intellectual and dream states. One of Tobasonakwut's favorite phrases is *andopawatchigan*, which means "seek your dream," but is lots more complicated. It means that first you have to find and identify your dream, often through fasting, and then that you also must carry out exactly what your dream tells you to do in each detail. And then the philosophy comes in, for by doing this repeatedly you will gradually come into a balanced relationship with all of life.

My experience with the language is of course very different. Instead of the language being beaten out of me, I've tried for years to acquire it. But how do I go back to a language I never had? I love my first language—why complicate my life with another? I will never have the facility to really use the flexible descriptive power of this language. Still, I love it. The sound comforts me. I feel as though all along this language was waiting for me with kindness. I imagine God hears this language. Perhaps my grandfather's use of the language penetrated. What the Ojibwe call the *Gizhe Mani-doo*, the ineffable and compassionate spirit residing in all that lives, is associated for me with the flow of Ojibwemowin. My Catholic training touched me intellectually and symbolically, but apparently never engaged my heart.

Ojibwemowin is one of the few surviving languages that evolved to the present here in North America. For an American writer, it seems crucial to at least have a passing familiarity with the language, which is adapted to the land as no other language can possibly be. Its philosophy is bound up in northern earth, lakes, rivers, forests, and plains. Its origins pertain to the animals and their particular habits, to the shades of meaning in the very placement of stones. Many of the names and songs associated with these places were revealed to people in dreams and songs—it is a language that most directly reflects a human involvement with the spirit of the land itself. It is the language of the paintings that seem to glow from within the rocks.

That is not to say Ojibwemowin is an elevated language of vanished spirituality. One of my favorite words is *wiindibaanens* or computer. It means "little brain machine." Ojibwe people have words for animals from other continents. *Genwaabiigigwed*, the long-necked horse, is a giraffe. *Ojaanzhingwedeyshkanaad*, rhinoceros, the one with the horn sticking out of his nose. *Nandookomeshiinh* is the lice hunter, the monkey. There are words for the serenity prayer used in twelve-step programs and translations of nursery rhymes. The varieties of people other than Ojibwe or Anishinabe are also named: *Aniibiishaabookewininiwag*, the tea people, are Asian. All Europeans are *Omakakiininiwag*, or frog people, but the French are *Wemitigoozhiwag*, the wooden-cross people. Catholics, who included the Jesuit priests, are *Mekadewikonayewininiwag*, the black-robe men. *Agongosininiwag*, the chipmunk people, are Scandinavian. I'm still trying to find out why.

When it comes to nouns, there are blessedly fewer of them and no designations of gender, no feminine or masculine possessives or articles. Nouns are mainly designated as animate or inanimate, though what is alive and dead doesn't correspond at all to what an English speaker might imagine. For instance, the word for stone, *asin*, is animate. After all, the preexistence of the world according to Ojibwe religion consisted of a conversation between stones. People speak to and thank the stones in the sweat lodge, where the asiniig are superheated and used for healing. They are addressed as grandmothers and grandfathers. Once I began to think of stones as animate, I started to wonder whether I was picking up a stone or it was putting itself into my hand. Stones are no longer the same as they were to me in English.

Ojibwemowin was of course a language of memory, an oral language, passed on by community but not written. For most of the last two centuries, missionized students adapted the English alphabet and wrote phonetically. Ojibwe orthography has recently been standardized so that the language can be taught in schools and universities. In this book, I have tried to use mainly accepted spellings, although I've fudged a little with Ojibwe words that might be confused with English words, and done my best on words that aren't in the *Concise Dictionary of Minnesota Ojibwe*, by Nichols and Nyholm. I've mastered shamefully little of the language. I'm still working on its most basic forms. Even if I do occasionally get a sentence right, there are so many dialects of Ojibwe that, for many speakers, I'll still have gotten it wrong. And yet, as ludicrous as my Ojibwe must sound to a fluent speaker, I have never, ever, been greeted with a moment of impatience or laughter. Perhaps people wait until I've left the room, but more likely, I think, there is an urgency about attempting to speak the language.

To native speakers like Tobasonakwut, the language is a deeply loved entity. A spirit or an originating genius belongs to each word. Before attempting to speak this language, students petition these spirits with gifts of cloth, tobacco, and food. Anyone who attempts Ojibwemowin is engaged in something more than learning tongue twisters. However awkward my nouns, unstable my verbs, however stumbling my delivery, to engage in the language is to engage the spirit

of the words. And as the words are everything around us, and all that we are, learning Ojibwemowin is a lifetime pursuit that might be described as living a religion.

Gigaa-waabamin

Ojibwe people don't say good-bye, that's too final. "I'll see you" is as close to good-bye as the language goes for a common parting. Some habits of Ojibwe have filtered into my English and I find that I can't say good-bye, or if I do,

I have to soften it with see-you-laters and have-funs and always, to my children and Tobasonakwut, drive-carefully. *Weweni,* careful. Or, as others jokingly say, *weweni babam-anadis,* which translates roughly as an admonition to be careful as you go around being ugly in your ugly life. Or *gego anooj igo ezhichigeken.* Don't do any of the weird things that I would. *Gigaa-waabamin* means "I'll see you again." That's just the way it is. He has a complicated life up north and I have a complicated life down in Minneapolis, so there is a lot of gigaa-waabamin.

4

Books

The Skylark Motel

Weary, Kiizhikok and I stop at a spot just off the highway, one of those square tubes of rooms facing the road. The line of identical brown doors and windows, like staring faces, has a sullen aspect. No skylarks. The texturized siding is a defeated looking tan color. There is a small office, dim but for a glowing television screen. The yard is dust, struggling weeds, trampled gravel. When looking for a small motel, I usually choose a place with window boxes, or at least a few flowers growing in a tractor tire filled with dirt, feeling hope rise at that small signal of care. But it's late, Kiizhikok is hungry, and I'm disoriented, as one always is leaving some wild place on the Earth and returning to human disorder. The unattractive nature of the towns and buildings seems purposeful. There is a belligerent streak to the ugliness. Or maybe I'm just tired. Here is an island, but of a very different sort.

The loneliness of roadside motels steals over me at once. Walking into my room, number 33, even with Kiizhikok's presence to cushion me, the sadness soaks up through my feet. True, I might have dreams here, these places always inspire uneasy nights and sometimes spectacular and even numinous dreams. But they test my optimism. My thoughts go dreary. The door shows signs of having been forced open. I can still see the crowbar marks where a lock was jimmied. And oh dear, it is only replaced with a push-in knob that can be undone with a library card, or any stiff bit of plastic, I think, as I don't suppose that someone intent on break-ing into room 33 would use a library card. Or if they did, I wonder, dragging in one duffle and the diaper bag, plus Kiizhikok football-style, would it be a good sign or a bad sign? Would it be better to confront an ill-motived intruder who was well read, or one indifferent to literature?

I rein my thoughts in, get my bearings. There are touch-es. Although the bed sags and the pickle-green coverlet is pilly and suspicious looking, the transparent sheets are tight and clean. A strangely evocative fall foliage scene is set above the bed—hand painted! Signed with a jerky black squiggle. The bathroom shower has a paper sanitary mat picturing a perky mermaid, breasts hidden by coils of green hair. The terrifying stain in the center of the carpet is almost covered with a woven rug. As always, on car trips where I will surely encounter questionable bedcovers, I've brought my own quilt. There is a bedside lamp with a sixty-watt bulb, and once Kiizhikok is asleep I can read.

Reading Sebald's *Austerlitz* in a cheap motel, insecure,

with a chair pushed beneath the doorknob and the drapes held shut with hair clips, is an experience for which I will always be grateful. Books. Why? For just such a situation. Marooned in this uneasy night, shaken by the periodic shudder of passing semi trucks, every sentence grips me. My brain holds onto each trailing line as though grasping a black rope in a threatening fog. I finish half a page, then read it over again, then read the next half of the page and then the entire page, twice. Not many books can be read with such intimacy, nor are there many so beautifully composed that the writing alone brings comfort. I carry *Middlemarch* along with me on book tours because the elaborate twists in George Eliot's sentences provoke in me a mood of concentrated calm.

Austerlitz is about the near dissolution of a man's personality during the reconstruction of his memory. Austerlitz, who has forgotten most of his early childhood, follows threads of history, traceries of his own consciousness; he digs through lists of deportees and examines photographs and propaganda movies to find the truth of his origins. He learns that he was sent on a children's transport from Prague to England at the beginning of World War II, and that his mother died in the humanly mechanized and phenomenally cruel "model ghetto" of Theresienstadt. He understands this slowly. The book moves minutely along this path toward knowledge, and seems at every sentence to deviate but always returns to the unfolding story. It is a very simple book, and unbearably profound. Page after page is about how history sinks into the mind, tormentingly sometimes, and what arrests and disturbances truth causes until finally the human heart can accept its sorrows, heal itself by enduring the unendurable, and go on beating.

The books we bring to strange places become guides and prevailing metaphors, catch-alls, lenses for new experience. As I read late into the night, moths whirling at the spotted shade, this book speaks to me with melancholy prescience, anticipating 9/11 in the first pages when Austerlitz speaks of how the smallest buildings—cottages, little pavilions— bring us peace, while we contemplate vast buildings, overdone buildings, with a wonder which is also dawning horror "for somehow we know by instinct that outsize buildings cast the shadow of their own destruction before them, and are designed from the first with an eye to their later existence as ruins." The description of the village of Llanwddyn, in Wales, submerged by the waters of a great reservoir, reminds me of the sensations I experience when talking to Tobasonakwut about the many settlements and cabins far out on Lake of the Woods, some of them drowned. Like Austerlitz, I too feel as though I've seen the vanished people walking, felt their eyes upon me, and that when I stare down into the opaque water, they are somehow calmly looking up from their ordinary tasks, which they have carried on, below us, for thousands of years.

I try to stay awake for as long as I can, getting up to wash my face at the rust-stained sink. Every time I turn on the tap unseen pipes clunk. Finally, one page sluices into the next and I start awake to find I have been holding my book upright, perhaps reading in my sleep, for I don't know if my eyes were even shut. And I wonder as I turn out the light and settle into the sagging mattress if my sleeping self understood what it read, and indeed, if I will ever know who I am during these dark hours? Asleep, we are strangers to ourselves. Sometimes, as now, it seems odd that we go on day after day accepting this great dislocation, growing used to it, trusting that our night self resembles our day self, that neither will betray the other come morning.

Kay-Nah-Whi-Wah-Nung

On Minn. 11 driving east toward the border crossing at International Falls, I see a large billboard that advertises "a gathering place of historical interest." Kah-Nah-Whi-Wah-Nung. I'm intrigued and as I have some time to dispose of, I decide to investigate. The road I am directed down is quite deserted, and for many miles I see only pastures, a few tawny brown cows, fence posts and gravel. Then suddenly I turn into a large parking lot filled with cars from as far away as Illinois and Florida. The place is still mysterious. From the lot I can see only a wooden door and part of a cedar shake roof. Upon entering the door, and facing a sudden and surprising curve of descending stairs, I understand I've come upon some sort of museum. As I walk down the long, wide, yellow stone staircase, the building opens into a cool, graceful, pleasant interior space divided into display sections, a book and craft shop, and an aquarium filled with live sturgeon, *namewag*.

I'm very glad to see the sturgeon close up, and watch them eagerly. They are, indeed, strangely ancient-looking with their rumpled snouts and whiskers. Their bellies are a cool off-white and their skins are gray, the color so soft, and they look painted. They are here, in this building, because the Rainy River Band of Ojibwe is raising and releasing them into the Rainy River. These young namewag are the size of large walleyes, but they may grow to be underwater giants, like the one that Kiizhikok and I saw at the Eternal Sands, or even bigger.

After looking through the displays of Ojibwe life and at the collections of artifacts, I treat myself to the gift shop. I find a number of handmade mocassins, the word is from the Ojibwe, usually spelled *makazinan*. These locally made makazinan are unusually fine, some made with brain-tanned moosehide, No. 13 beads or cut beads, and lined with blanket material or rabbit fur. I pick out several pairs, and then find a book of poems, *Spirit Horses*, by an Ojibwe poet I admire named Al Hunter. The woman who handles the sale proudly tells me that she's Al's niece, and that he happens to be downstairs.

I point out my name on the back cover of Al's book, a blurb. Al comes upstairs and we sit down in the little café which serves fresh, beautiful, Ojibwe-influenced wild rice soups, casseroles, fruit salads. We drink the ubiquitous iced tea of this part of Canada. Al and his partner Sandra recently completed a walk around Lake Superior to draw attention to its pollution. That's a long walk. Al says the days merged, and that time was beautiful. He works for his band, Rainy River Ojibwe, on a land claim that has had promising results—so far, this center, which is located on land containing huge burial mounds restored to the tribe, is one of those results. He tells me something very striking. He says that when he returned home after his education, to work, there were many terrible and pressing needs to address on his reserve—poverty, alcoholism, despair—so he called a meeting. At this meeting, he needed to tell people there was something that their reserve gravely needed. A library.

Books. Why?

Because they are wealth, sobriety, and hope.

Al's reserve now has a library bought with tribal contributions and slowly filling with books.

The Border Crossing

I try not to be nervous, but I can't help it—I am carrying those eagle spikes and although I have a right to carry them and I have my band enrollment card, I hate the questioning, the scrutiny, the suspicious nature of the border guards. What I don't expect is that the man, my age, very trim and professional looking in his blue uniform, will question me about my baby.

"Do you have any proof that you're her mother?"

I stare at him in shock, it is such a strange question. I have to think.

"Well," I say, "I can nurse her."

He stares back at me. Gestures to the side of a building. "Pull over."

Am I going to be required to nurse my baby in front of some border-crossing guard? I pull over, wishing that I had a copy of the Jay Treaty, which guarantees Native People the right to cross the Canadian–U.S. border without hassle. A woman meets me. I undergo more questioning. I start to grip Kiizhikok a little harder, in alarm I suppose, and in response she holds onto me tightly. The guard asks a series of easy questions and then, suddenly, as though to trip me up, shoots the question, "And who is this?" at me, indicating Kiizhikok. Each time, grasping the strategy, I shoot right back, "My daughter!" Each time, Kiizhikok grips me even tighter. I'm so glad she isn't going through one of those mother-rejecting stages, or branching out adventurously, or growling at me, as she likes to do as a joke, right now. Eventually, the sharp-eyed woman clears us. We've passed some mother/daughter test. But when I get into the van I find that I'm actually shaken. For the first time in quite a while I'm surprised to find that I crave a stiff drink. Yes, I do. A straight shot of really good whiskey. And a cigarette.

"What have they done to me?" I say out loud, buckling her in, giving her the baby cell phone *and* the Chinese blender *and* her sippy cup, then buckling myself in and guzzling water from a plastic bottle. It's time to get out of International Falls and back onto a lake.

Meeting Up Again

Once again there is this meeting-up uncertainty. I am supposed to rendezvous with members of the Lac Court Oreilles Ojibwe Language Society. We are going to stay together at an island on Rainy Lake among Ernest Oberholtzer's thousands of books. There was a phone call, a plan, a lost cell phone number, a time to meet. The words Super Stop or Stop and Super or One Stop or Super Shop and Save. Immediately after hanging up I should have written down the name of the meeting place! As I enter International Falls I am more and more confused by the similarity of gas station stop names and supermarkets. They seem to have the same name in various combinations. I make a slow examination of each one, but don't find my friends. Finally, I haul Kiizhikok out and we do a magnificent shopping at a place called Super One. We buy fresh cherries and all the makings for a corn stew and for an innovative type of trail mix that we have developed on this trip—one that includes salted nuts, pecans, figs, cinnamon chips, and golden raisins. We buy milk, lettuce, and a box of arrowroot baby crackers. Slowly, we walk the aisles, waiting for our friends, until I realize that in one-half hour I have to meet the boat that will take us out to the island.

As it turns out, it was just lateness, an Ojibwe trait so common it is not considered a failing. I'm relieved to see that everyone is gathering and consolidating gear once I go out to the point from which we will embark. My particular friends are a young couple with a baby boy just Kiizhikok's age. They are Ojibwe teachers and very passionate about the language. They speak only Ojibwe to their son, and to my baby, too. She understands them and has quite a few Ojibwe words. Her shoes are *maki* for makizanan and her water is *nibi,* but we have a long way to go before sentence structure. We are going to drive out in a pontoon boat steered by the caretaker of the island, a very agreeable, sunny-haired woman from Ames, Iowa, named Mary Holmes.

Years ago, Mary fell in love with the island of the books, became a caretaker of that island, and is now on the board of the small foundation that administers a tiny trust and takes care of the estate that belonged to Ernest Oberholtzer. The trust allows a few small groups to visit the ecologically fragile island. Because Ernest Oberholtzer was a close friend to the Ojibwe, the foundation honors that relationship by allowing teachers and serious students of the language, as well as one or two Ojibwe writers, to visit on retreats. Most people who come to Ober's island more than a few times become working members of the loose conglomerate of people who support the place in one way or another. It is the kind of place that inspires a certain energy that I can only term "Oberholtzerian"—a combination of erudition, conservationism, nativism, and exuberant eccentricity. Perhaps, I think, the air of Tinkertoy idealism here has something to do with the confluence of fascinations that occurs when Germans and Ojibwe people mix. This place reminds me quite a bit of my own family.

Ernest Oberholtzer

He was born in 1884, grew up in an upper middle-class home in Davenport, Iowa, suffered a bout of rheumatic fever that weakened his heart. He went to Harvard, where he made friends with bookish people like Conrad Aiken and Samuel Eliot Morison. His heart kept bothering him. Told by a doctor he had just one year to live, he decided to spend it in a canoe. He traveled three thousand miles in a summer. Paddling a canoe around the Rainy Lake watershed and through the Quetico-Superior wilderness was just the thing for his heart, so he kept on paddling. He lived to be ninety-three years old.

Ernest Oberholtzer packed those years with passions and enthusiasms, ceaseless physical activity, and loving friendships. He never married, though he lived on his island with a woman who supported him and apparently would have liked to tie the knot. He was trained to play the classical violin and he loved literature, book collecting, landscape architecture, bike travel, and photographing moose. The greatest political act of his life was to take on the massive lumber companies and save the Boundary Waters, the Quetico-Superior wilderness, I hope for all time. His friendships with the Ojibwe were abiding, he was a devoted and very curious companion. He was attracted to the unknown, to great deeds, and exploration.

In 1912, at the age of twenty-eight, he persuaded an extremely capable fifty-year-old Ojibwe man, Taytahpaswaywitong, Billy Magee, to accompany him on an expedition that he hoped would make his name as an explorer. He intended to travel the Barrens bounded by Lake Winnipeg, Hudson Bay, and Reindeer Lake. The area was unmapped, unknown, unexplored since Samuel Hearne's 1770 expedition. They were, of course, going by canoe.

Oberholtzer wasn't much of a hunter, so they had to pack an inordinate amount of food—seven hundred pounds. Every portage consisted of five round-trips. They had a small window of opportunity before the lakes and rivers would freeze solid, stranding them, and so began their journey in late June. By August they would experience freezing nights and woodlands covered in frost. By September, October, and at last November, they would be paddling for their lives. Filling in blanks on the map by using a compass and watch that his mother had given him, Ober mapped the terrain through which they passed. They paddled steadily, and thereby estimated distances hour by hour. Often lost, they desperately navigated mazey lakes, ultimately Nueltin, or Sleeping Island Lake, searching for a river called Thiewiaza that would deliver them in a path toward Hudson Bay.

Loneliness, anxiety, and the strangeness of the lake itself worked on Oberholtzer and at times his journal entries took on a desperate, dreamy quality. On the Barrens, the men hallucinated, lost themselves, but managed to plunge on. Ober saw trees as city smokestacks, people who weren't there. Ever after, the journey was to haunt Ober and remain mysterious to others. At one point he climbed an esker and left in a can a note with his last words. In his journal, Ober notes that Billy Magee would tell him how, every night, he talked in his sleep or made horrible noises. The two came down the side of Hudson Bay. They missed the last steamer out of the country to run before the lakes and rivers froze over, and so they headed south just a hair before winter, freezing all the way and paddling fourteen hours at a stretch, often through the night, their feet and legs stuffed all around with wild hay. Incredibly, they paddled until the first week of November, through snow, along the shore of Lake Winnipeg, and at last made the small settlement of Gimli, Manitoba. There, the two beached their canoe, got haircuts, and returned to the world. They had been paddling and portaging non-stop, often deep into the night, since June 25.

It was a grueling, original, life-changing feat. Though Ober lectured on the trip, he never managed to write about it. Joe Paddock observes in *Keeper of the Wild*:

> Though a conflicted desire to do so haunted him into old age, Ober would never publish or even complete a written account of the Hudson Bay trip. Over the years, whenever he did try to write of it he was overwhelmed with emotion. One is reminded of Meriwether Lewis's inability to write of his great wilderness adventure. As with Lewis, Ober's careful journal of the trip may in itself be the significant book he hoped would one day tell his tale.

That book, *Toward Magnetic North*, has recently been published along with many of the extraordinary photographs that Ober took of the places and of the people he encountered. His photographs of a family of Inuit hunters who took them in and guided them at the northernmost reach of their voyage are the most remarkable. In one, an ancient woman, probably about my age, is framed by a huge stack of wood on her back. She drags herself along or rights herself with two sticks. Another, of a ten-year-old boy to whom his father gave the pipe Ober offered the family as a gift, smokes that pipe gazing with shrewd and thoughtful economy into a familiar distance.

Ober's House and Ober's Books

On reaching the island, I find I am the last to choose a place to stay. I'm thrilled to find that no one else has decided to sleep at Oberholtzer's house. Though each cabin has its own charm, I've always wanted to stay at Oberholtzer's. I want to stay among what I imagine must have been his favorite books. The foundation has tried to keep the feeling of Ober's world intact, and so the books that line the walls of his loft bedroom were pretty much the ones he chose to keep there, just hundreds out of more than 11,000 on the island. Heavy on Keats, I notice right off, as we enter. Volumes of both the poems and letters. Lots of Shakespeare. A gorgeously illustrated copy of *Leaves of Grass*. In some shelves in an alcove above the bed, curious volumes on sexuality including Kraft-Ebbing. I take down one work entitled *Sin and Sex*, and find that an old letter has been used as a bookmark. I read the letter, which is from Oberholtzer to his mother. The subject of the letter is the stock market. Oh well. I replace the letter in the book. Kiizhikok and I spread our quilts on the bed and then we lie down to admire the view from the bed, straight down a rocky channel into a lovely little bay.

Both of the islands next to this one, also owned by the foundation, are kept wild. This island, Mallard, is planted with cheerful care—pink petunias in bark planters. Baskets of salmon impatiens. Tiny perennial gardens of daisies and lilies are set against stone walls. It has seven cabins and two outhouses. But to call the buildings cabins and the privies outhouses is completely inadequate. To start with, Oberholtzer's house is built against the side of a rock and rises three full stories with a surprise sleeping cupola on top, a secret room that can be reached only through a ladder leading into what looks like a chimney. For handles, the sturdy riveted doors are fitted with pieces of curved driftwood, or antlers. The very first floor, the kitchen, is reached either through a trapdoor from above, or an outside screen door above stone steps that lead directly down into the lake. Next to the kitchen door, against the cool of another rock wall, an ice house is set, disguised by vines that loop over a pale turquoise door. I love this door-leading-into-the-stone-hill. I have photographed it many times. There is a Japanese

teahouse at the end of the island. To reach it, one crosses an arched stone bridge. Another set of stone steps leads into what is called The Roman Bath—a deep tub of silky lake. There is The Birdhouse, rising like a Seuss concoction into the pines, story after story, with a zigzag of steps and ladders. As the other cabins are, it's heated with a tiny woodstove. There is one more house, made like the others of unpeeled cedar logs, there is a library cabin, which I'll get to, and there are the outhouses. Mine is built with a tiny step up, a perfect screen door, a lovely window, and a long view down the center of the channel facing east.

WE CONVENE TO eat in an old early twentieth-century cook's barge used by lumber companies to feed their crews as they ravaged the northern old-growth trees and floated the logs down to the sawmills. Ober had this cook's barge hauled onto his island. An old bell signals meals. Original plates and dishes of every charm—Depression glass, milk glass, porcelains, and sweet old flowery unmatched Royal Doulton china dishes—crowd the open shelves. A cabin just out front of the cook's barge, hauled here too, was once a floating whorehouse, I am told. Now it houses a piano, and three neat beds. A child has written a sign, tacked to its wall, that advises visitors not to be alarmed if they see things they are unprepared to see—like spirits. There is supposed to be a spirit family that inhabits this island.

I'll tell you right off, I don't see hide nor hair of the spirits. But I can't speak for Kiizhikok, with her still open fontanel. They might be talking to her. Or singing her to sleep. Because she sleeps on this island, takes naps of an unprecedented length and then tumbles into sleep beside me as I read long into the night. There is a fever that overcomes a book-lover who has limited time to spend on Ober's island. A fever to read. Or at least to open the books. There is no question of finishing or even delving deeply. I have only days. Among the books, I feel what is almost a low swell of grief, a panic.

Once the baby is asleep I vault to Ober's shelves. I first wash and dry my hands—I just have to. Really, I suppose I should be wearing gloves. Then with a kind of bingeing greed I start, taking one book off the shelf, sucking what I can of it in, replacing it. This goes on for as many hours as I can stand. G. K. Chesterton on William Blake. *Ben Jonson's Works in Four Volumes*, Oxford University, 1811. *Where The Blue Begins* by Christopher Morley, illustrated by Arthur Rackham, first edition and first printing. An 1851 copy of *The House of the Seven Gables*. And *The Voyages of Peter Esprit Radisson, Being an Account of His Travels and Experiences Among the North American Indians*. A wonderful volume, more recent than most, published in 1943 and transcribed from original manuscripts in the British Museum. I keep reading this last book until, late at night, the loons in full cry, my mosquito coil threading citronella smoke, I have to quit. Knowing that I must be alert enough tomorrow to feed Kiizhikok and take the stones from her mouth, I force myself to sleep. But as I drift away with her foot in my hand I am led to picture an alternate life.

In my imagined life, there is an enchanted interlude. All children are given a year off from school to do nothing but read (I don't know if they'd actually like this, but in my fantasy my daughters are exquisitely happy). We come to this island. One year is given to me, also, to read. I am not allowed to write. I am forced to do nothing but absorb Oberholtzer's books. Every day, I pluck down stacks of books from the shelves upon shelves tacked up on every wall and level of each of the seven cabins on Ober's island. Slowly, I go through the stacks, reading here and there until I find the book of which I must read every word. Then I do read every word, beneath a very bright lamp. When my brain is stuffed my daughters and I go swimming, play poker, or eat. Life consists of nothing else.

Ober and Moose

I find some lovely photographs of moose among the archives—Oberholtzer took them. Tracking down, sneaking up on, and photographing moose was a big passion with him. His guide, companion, and mentor, Billy Magee or Taytahpaswaywitong, thought Ober just a little strange, but went along with it, bringing him to within feet of some of the shiest and orneriest creatures of the lake. The photographs that resulted were the first such ever taken of the animal, and Oberholtzer became known as a great expert. *Keeper of the Wild* makes use of notes that Ober took on those photography trips. I think, of course, of the three young female moose we saw in Lake of the Woods, those awkward young beauties cavorting in the reeds, and so innocent about our approach. Ober wrote beautifully about a similarly trusting young bull:

Inch by inch, scarcely moving, Billy propelled the canoe forward, while I knelt in the bow, camera in hand. The sun was fiercely hot, there was only a breath of breeze. The little bull several times raised his head to gaze at us wonderingly; and each time Billy stopped paddling. Thus, during the moments when the moose's head was submerged, we advanced till we were only twenty feet away. The bull edged off a foot or so, turned his back, and suddenly faced around again, whined ever so slightly like a dog and at last, after a moment's reflection, dipped his head under water. I was itching to take his picture, but I noticed something remarkable. Instead of immersing his head completely, as is the custom of the moose when feeding, he left half his long ears protruding. He was *listening*; and I was afraid that, if I clicked the shutter, he would scamper away. When he raised his head again, however, I decided to chance it. I clicked. He flinched, moved away a step again and then resumed his feeding. He seemed completely reassured, for I noticed now that even the tips of his ears were under water. We were still gliding nearer. I took another picture, a third, one after another. At last, lo and behold, the little fellow got down on his knees on the river bottom, and for a second or so his body was wholly lost to sight. His head came up first, with ears pricked. He shook it and the ears flapped drolly against his cheeks. When he rose, he looked at us inquiringly, almost mischievously, with his languid brown eyes. His shaggy winter coat was still clinging in patches to his hindquarters. . . . To my great surprise he calmly stepped toward us and sniffed with his long snout; and I could have touched him with the paddle. But Billy, always cautious and respectful toward a moose, backed the canoe a few strokes. Thus for fifteen minutes we played with this strange neighbor.

Feasting

The blueberries, *miinan*, have ripened on the island. The first thing Kiizhikok does the next morning is crouch low to the berry bushes and stuff herself with miinan. I show her how. This is the one traditional Ojibwe pursuit I'm good at. Now, before Kiizhikok picks and eats all of the blueberries, it is time to feast the first ripening. Rose Tainter, a traditional elder from Lac Court Oreilles, prays in Ojibwemowin, with her sacred pipe, at breakfast. We have a huge bowl of blueberries. A spirit dish is prepared. The dish is made up of small portions of the food we'll eat, with tobacco set alongside the portions. The spirit dish is either left outside for the spirits or burned as an offering. This is the way the Ojibwe have always given thanks for the first berries of the year. After Rose has finished praying and the spirit dish is

set outside, we eat. We eat seriously. We eat with attention. We eat with a lot of laughing.

It seems to me that Ojibwe people always eat with happy grace. Food is part of every gathering and ceremony. Even our weekly meetings to learn the language are based around a potluck dinner, mainly centered around casseroles heavy on wild rice. Today on Ober's island, breakfast consists of pancakes and Ojibwe maple syrup, scrambled eggs, fresh walleye breaded and fried, a hash of potatoes and crisp turnips, and a big bowl of blueberries. There is also lots more fruit on the side, coffee, and black tea. We'll have a big lunch just a couple hours after the breakfast dishes are cleared and washed. And then dinner, which might involve venison sausage, more walleye, boiled cabbage and potatoes, or if we are lucky enough to see Nancy Jones, whatever she has hunted might appear.

Nancy Jones, Ogimaawigwanebiik, happens to be one of the most extraordinary women I know.

For starters, she holds the world record as the quickest beaver skinner. I don't know where, exactly, she earned the World's Quickest Beaver Skinner title, but I'm assured this is the truth. She makes a few judicious cuts and turns the animal inside out. It's like sleight of hand. Nancy does exquisite beadwork, placing each tiny cut bead just so on makazinan of smoked moosehide, trimmed with otter fur, lined with blanket. Nancy has a great laugh and deep spiritual knowledge, she is an Ojibwe language teacher, and fiercely devoted to Ojibwe culture. Her children are language teachers, too, and she has taught them her bush skills. Still, they are amazed at her fortitude and endurance. Nancy has been known to kill, skin, and cart back to her cabin a whole moose *and* a deer in one day. She can snare rabbits, trap anything from lynx to pine marten. She can shoot the head off a partridge sitting in a tree, and probably catch the partridge as it falls, too. Ojibwe are meat eaters, that's just how it is. The joke goes: What is an Ojibwe vegetarian called? A poor hunter. Nevertheless, it was Nancy's deer haunch and a fat string of bass three years ago that changed my then youngest daughter, Aza, from a supermarket carnivore to a thoughtful vegetarian.

It was either the deer haunches, or the ribs. Anyway, on our last visit to Ober's island, Aza made a decision from which she has never deviated. I was amazed that a ten-year-old could decide with such conviction. She won't even eat a fish after she went to the dock to check on Nancy's stringer. Later, she said to me that one of the fish had looked up at her. That did it. I must have been a hard-hearted little person, because as the granddaughter of a pair of butchers I helped kill chickens and watched from a corner of the slaughter-house as my uncle knocked sheep, shot cows, scalded and gutted dead pigs. And yet it has taken my daughter Aza to make me really attempt anything like a consistently veg-etarian set of habits, and it started out purely because I felt bound to support her tenderness on behalf of animals.

At any rate, although killing and eating wild game is for the Ojibwe a spiritual as well as delectable enterprise, there is no vegetarianism this year on Ober's island. Nancy and her son Pebaamibines are running an Ojibwe language camp this summer on her land, about a forty-five-minute boat ride from Ober's island. They come to stay for a night, but all the game is left at the language camp and so we eat the most incredible spaghetti bolognese. Maybe it's the red pepper flakes in the sauce, or the type of onion. Maybe it's the air. Maybe it's the mosquitoes, and how we are free of them in the well-screened kitchen.

Nancy remembers Ernest Oberholtzer very well—he made eggs for her family on their first visit, when they pad-dled over and tied their canoe to his dock. In Oberholtzer's photo archive there are dozens of pictures of Nancy's family, her late husband's family, and of Nancy as a child, strong-minded looking even then, grinning, wearing a soft red woolen hat. Pebaamibines touches a picture on the wall. I recognize it as a photograph of Billy Magee. The man who guided and paddled with Oberholtzer on the great 1912 ad-venture is a close ancestor.

Maang

A hot wind blows over the island, and Kiizhikok and I are in and out of the water all afternoon. We edge ourselves carefully down a stone stairway into the cool tea-colored water of Rainy Lake. Pushing off, we float together, into the channel, sighing in dreamy relief. We bob along in our life jackets, talking part Ojibwe, part English, and part mother-baby nonsense. The world is perfect. The shadows are long but on the rocks they still burn like iron. The sun's a fierce gold. Baby and I watch the silhouette of a big loon approach down the channel between islands. It comes nearer and nearer, as silent as we are. Then the *maang* is abnormally close, closer, too close, and again I am filled with the now familiar sense of uneasy assessment. That beak looks sharp! Will it peck Kiizhikok? The loon's eyes are very red! But the loon isn't going to poke my baby, of course, it only circles, coming close enough for us to count the white spots on its back and regard the spectral pupil of its weird reflective eye.

Again, I marvel how animals seem attracted to the baby, and once we have emerged from the water and are drying off in the light breeze, I ask Nancy Jones if she saw the loon swimming with us. I ask modestly, sure that she'll tell me that Kiizhikok has some unusual power to attract maang.

"*Geget*, I saw it," she says casually. "He liked your life jackets."

Our life jackets?

"They're red. That's how we used to catch loons and eat them," Nancy says. "We used red things. They'll come close

and investigate anything red." Then she adds, "We don't eat them anymore."

"How did they use to taste?" I ask her.

"Rich," she says.

The Library

I am haunted by a book that I found the first time I visited Ober's island. It was stuck away in a corner of a little cabin I haven't described, one devoted to books alone, the library. My find was a little pamphlet-sized inconsequential-looking book covered with a black paper that looked like oilcloth. I slipped it from the shelf and opened it. *Tristram Shandy*. One of the first novels in the English language. As it was originally published in serial form this was but a portion of the first edition and first printing. Laurence Sterne had signed the title page. I had a strange, covetous, Gollum-like feeling as I held the book, *my precious*. I suppose it was the beginning of the sort of emotional response to books that drives those collectors you hear about, occasionally, to fill their apartments with books until there are only book tunnels to walk through and the floors eventually collapse down onto their neighbors.

Of course, I have to see *Tristram Shandy* again. I want to visit this book, and also to make sure I really saw it. But this time I can't find the book although I crawl with Kiizhikok on hands and knees looking for likely places it could have been stashed. Its absence bothers me. Although I'm helplessly in the grip of other books now, and currently in love with a corny purple edition of Catlin's journals, I keep sneaking around the bottom of the shelf where I found my precious, peeking over other books, behind the shelves, like a dog sure that it will find a bone hidden years before.

Mary Holmes goes through the catalog with me, and that particular volume isn't mentioned. Which doesn't mean, she tells me, that it wasn't actually there. So I might have seen it. This is, for me, like a birder having possibly photographed an ivorybill then losing the film. I'm chagrined—why didn't I do something about the book? Show it to someone? Make certain it was cared for? But I know that the answer is that I didn't because I am in somewhat uneasy agreement with the spirit of the island, which is to let the books exist as they were meant to exist, to be read, to be found and then unfound. To have their own life. Somehow, that also puts me in conflict with a piece of my heart. For I also want the books to be protected from people like me, whose itch to hold them might overwhelm even the strictest conscience. Even now, I can feel it, the line is thin. Especially when you can't find *Tristram Shandy*.

Signed, goddamnit, I'm positive!

Mary tells me that Ober had left no will regarding the island and his books and cabins, so that ten years passed while all of the legalese was sorted out. During those years, the books were alone. I brood on this. The books. Alone in the cold and through the humid summers, alone in the cabins for ten years as roofs collapsed, alone as squirrels invaded and dismantled eighteenth-century bindings to line their nests with rare pages. I am afflicted with such melancholy at the thought of the books all alone on the island that I have to walk back to Ober's house, to nap with Kiizhikok, to settle my mind. This whole island, filled with books, and no one to care for them! I would have liked to have been here. I imagine it as something like living in a great Cornell Box, only while

Joseph Cornell's visual themes were white spheres and tiny glasses and peeling cubicles and star maps that suggested vast compressions of time and space, here the themes would be the books, the words stacked endlessly. Spine to spine, margin to margin. Peeling, curling, waiting in a thrilling passivity for someone—like me!

There was an original Edward Curtis portfolio of portraits of American Indians among the books. I'm glad that I don't know what else. Some of the most valuable were sold once the little foundation of Oberholtzer's friends and supporters was formed. In a panic of retrieval, some were bought back. But a piece of the careful intention and depth of Ober's collection was lost. Still, the collection is for me both a caution and an inspiration. It is surely a good thing that Oberholtzer devoted only a portion of his vast energy to book collecting. He was a dedicated bibliophile, careful and disciplined, ordering books from London booksellers with great specificity and detail, and receiving notes and invoices in return, some of which are still tucked into the pages of his books. Nicholas Basbane's wonderful book on book obsession, *A Gentle Madness*, begins with a description of the difference between the bibliophile and the bibliomaniac:

With thought, patience, and discrimination, book passion becomes the signature of a person's character. When out of control and indulged to excess, it lets loose a fury of bizarre behavior. "The bibliophile is the master of his books, the bibliomaniac their slave," the German bibliographer Hanns Bohatta steadfastly maintained, though the dividing line can be too blurry to discern. Whatever the involvement, however, every collector inevitably faces the same harsh reality. After years spent in determined pursuit, a moment arrives when the precious volumes must pass to other shelves. Some accept the parting with calm and foresight; others ignore it entirely. Some erect grand repositories as monuments to their taste, others release their treasures with the whispered hope that they reach safe harbor in the next generation.

Whatever Oberholtzer's intentions were, I'm happy that his island is still filled with the books he pursued and acquired. Other than actual writing, the books a person leaves behind reflect most accurately the cast of that person's mind. If his spirit is with the spirit family living on the island, as some believe, then I'm sure that Ober misses his chief treasures, but feels relieved that the collection is more or less intact. For his assemblage does reflect his character, as the best collections do. His books on exploration, the great north of Canada and the Arctic, and his painstakingly procured works on Native American life, as well as the volumes of poetry he so loved and the works in German and the books on music, probably reflect as much as anyone can know of him.

Ober and the Ojibwe

One of the reasons, I think, that Ober so loved and was fascinated by the Ojibwe is that he loved the books in the people. He loved the oral tradition of storytelling, where the person becomes the book as in *Fahrenheit 451*. His Ojibwe name, Aadizookaan, means traditional story. As Pebaamibines tells it, Oberholtzer was always entering a circle of Ojibwe asking eagerly, "Aadizookaan? Aadizookaan?" And so, as Ojibwe do, he was affectionately nicknamed. He recorded several stories but never did complete a collection, or indeed, write the books he meant to about the Ojibwe. He hadn't, perhaps, the degree of passivity it takes to actually sit down and write a book. Or he hadn't the patience, maybe, to sit down long at all. His phenomenally active life benefited his Ojibwe friends in many ways, not the least of which is in the area of conservation, and now, in the ongoing hospitality that the board of the Oberholtzer Foundation has shown toward Ojibwe people, Ojibwe writers and language teachers, storytellers. During this retreat to the island, for instance, I am able both to take notes for this book and to work with Keller Paap and Lisa LaRonge on details of the first book that our nascent publishing house, Birchbark Books, will publish. It is a book by a gentle and deeply knowledgeable Ojibwe elder named Nawiigiizis. Ober definitely would have added this book to his collection, and as I leave I promise to send it, and this one, too, up north to the island of books.

5

Home

Telephone

We're going to make the drive straight down to the Cities
without stopping, so I keep Kiizhikok awake throughout the
last morning on the island, until we are on the road. To keep
her eyes open just a little longer, I break out a toy called
Alpha-Bug, who says, "hey, that tickles," when she's turned
on. Press the Alpha-Bug's feet and she says a letter and can
also make the sound of the letter. You can even get her to
say whole words, though not suggestive or swear words. My
older daughters have discovered that Alpha-Bug won't even
say the word "sex." How did they do that? These toys made
with sound chips did not exist when my other children were
young. Kiizhikok happily presses green plastic bug feet until
twenty miles south of International Falls, when the letter *D*
puts her to sleep.

I have only been in sporadic phone contact with my
daughters during this trip, which causes me great anxiety.

I know they are fine—as they are teenagers they each have a life project they're embarked on. One is making a film in London, one is studying in the Berkshires, one daughter is part of an international choir. Oddly, it has been easiest to talk to my daughter in London. I sat on a polished log chair at the one radio phone available on Ober's island, and she stood at a phone booth just outside King's College, using a phone card. We compared notes on food. She had found it best to frequent a Greek deli near the school instead of relying on cafeteria sandwiches made of mashed corn and chicken. I had found it best, in Canada, to rely on a trail mix heavy on dried fruit, except of course for the memorable lunch at Kay-Nah-Chi-Wah-Nung and the food shared with Ojibwe food-lovers on Ober's Island.

Now, as I merge just past Cloquet, Minnesota, onto 35 South heading back to Minneapolis, the little cell phone I've taken, silent all along, makes a triumphant tootling sound at the end of its plug-in cord. I start dialing, and talk to my daughters from the road, check in with my household and with my bookstore people, with my sisters and parents. All of a sudden I am back in the web of connection.

I am on the mainland, dry land, off the islands. Or so I think.

Return

We arrive. We return. Home is familiar and it is disorienting. For days, I'm not quite here and not quite there, but muddle around trying to enter the stream of my life. There is a sad discovery. The city forester has painted a blazing red ring and the letter *A*, sign of doom, around Old Stalwart's trunk. This tree is older than the house, and I've carefully had it treated with a protective fungicide every few years to discourage Dutch Elm disease. The treatment doesn't always work. I knew that. But it's like a friend of mine is stricken. The tree is the classic fluted shape and raises immense and graceful arms high above our three-story house. I love elm trees—grooved bark and sawtooth leaves and fluted silhouette. I think the Earth has chosen to praise the sky by growing this tree.

Even I can see the flags, the stunted and dead leaves, the ailing branches, the signs. I stand outside with the tree, in a state of helplessness—there should be a word specifically for the feeling one has about the death of a tree. I think of photographing Old Stalwart, but I can't bear to. Within days, the city tree crew arrives and saws off those long sweet limbs, lest the disease spread. I'm so sad I cannot look at the tree anymore, it hurts to see it maimed like that. A few more days pass and then the forester seals off the street, notches the rest of the tree, and fells the three-story-high stump onto the asphalt. I watch it go, with Kiizhikok, and feel the shock of its passage, a resounding shudder of the earth that tingles in our feet. That's it. It is gone. This has been a warm winter and a record number of elms have succumbed, as the deep cold helps kill off the beetles that spread the sickness. As I am finishing this book, the city stump grinder arrives and by the end of the day his rotary blade has turned the rest of

Old Stalwart into a pile of chips. It will be another hundred years, if the house survives this long, before a tree grown in its place tops the roofline and teases the sky.

Reading Distance

My happiness in being an older mother surprises me—though often worn out I don't seem to mind my sleepy days. I know they quickly pass. Some changes are permanent, though, for instance my middle-aged vision. The first time I held Kiizhikok in my arms, just after she was born, I looked into her perfect face and realized that I couldn't make out her features. I had to adjust her to my reading distance.

It occurs to me, now, that I now do this constantly. If reading is taken to mean comprehending, I step back often. I focus; to my great relief, I have a little more patience. I have learned to appreciate as well as to fear the swift current of hours. Those first jagged months of ceaseless exhaustion passed like dreams, so quickly I feel I've flown in and out of clouds. Already she is making sense of things and I am making sense of her. At the same time, my oldest daughters are soon leaving for college. All this year I have found myself sorting through photographs as though to persuade myself that their childhoods have actually happened, that all of those years really occurred in fabulous particularity.

Returning home, after a long anticipated trip, always does this to me. Time seems foreshortened, furiously spent, a blur. If, as Austerlitz says, time is by far the most artificial of all our inventions, then what am I living in, what is this force that holds me captive in its ineluctable continuance? As I still have *Austerlitz* to finish on my first night home, the book becomes a reassuring messenger from the near past, familiar now, a witness to my travels.

Austerlitz doesn't wear a watch, I am happy to read, considering one "a thoroughly mendacious object." I don't wear a watch either, unless forced by circumstance. He explains what I have never completely thought out about my hope of somehow resisting time through these little forms of protest. Austerlitz hopes, he says, that time will not pass away, has not passed away, that he can turn back and go behind it and there find everything as it once was. I suppose that is the point of sifting through my shoeboxes of photographs. Perhaps that is the point of everything, this writing most of all.

There is a surprise memory for me at the end of *Austerlitz*, one that simultaneously revives a forgotten person, a teacher of mine, and gives me an unexpected metaphor to use in understanding where we have been. The last pages of the book are about another book, a memoir by Dan Jacobson, a writer whose father, a Lithuanian rabbi, died in 1920 and caused his wife to decide to emigrate with her nine children to South Africa. They were the only people in his family who survived the Holocaust. Jacobson spent most of his childhood in the town of Kimberly, near the diamond mines, which were not fenced off and to the edge of which children ventured to look down into a depth of several thousand feet. As Dan Jacobson was my advisor during what seemed a very long term of study at University College, London, in 1976, I can almost see him describe how it was terrifying to see such emptiness open up a foot away from firm ground, to realize that there was no transition, only this dividing line, with ordinary life on one side and its unimaginable opposite on the other. The chasm into which no ray of light could penetrate, writes the narrator of *Austerlitz*, was Jacobson's image of the vanished past of his family and his people which, as he knows, can never be brought up from those depths again.

Dan Jacobson was a very kind man. I remember that as we talked, perhaps to set me at ease, for I was shy, he used to share chunks of the Cadbury bars he kept in his desk drawer—the kind in the purple wrapper, studded with chunks of nuts and raisins. How odd it seems now that he is with me in Minneapolis, and that I am nodding as I think, yes, it is as though when I look past a generation or into the past of Tobasonakwut's world there is a lightlessness, too, for nine of every ten native people perished of European diseases, leaving only diminished and weakened people to encounter what came next—the aggressions of civilization including government policies and missionaries and residential schools. Yet, here, as I turn to Kiizhikok sprawled in sleep beside me, is a light.

Wood Ticks

A pure little light, I think, reaching over to touch her curls. That is when I find the wood tick. It is still on the move, not attached, which is good. I pluck it away and dispose of it and make certain there are no more. This one was probably carried in on a shirt or blanket. Suddenly, of course, I itch all over. I don't know why they are so much worse than mosquitoes, for instance, but they *are* worse. Or maybe I just have a thing about them. Back on the island while eating lunch with Tobasonakwut, I plucked one off and made a shuddering noise. He opened the top layer of his sandwich and said, "throw him in." When I was a child and visited my grandparents in the Turtle Mountains, we cousins had wood-tick contests at the end of the day, after playing in the woods. Any number under twenty was scorned. I remember one cousin winning one night with a grand total of fifty-six. In the full blush of their season I've seen them swarm toward you off willow branches—swarm slowly. That's what's so awful. Their tiny, blood-drawn, implacable lust.

Up close, they are so small and neatly made. Of course, their true awfulness becomes apparent when they vampirize and grow big. Earlier this summer, about a week after bringing our dog back from a trip up north, Kiizhikok brought me a huge tick she'd found, fallen off the dog. She held it solemnly, pinched carefully between her thumb and first finger, her pinky crooked. Its legs, fine as copper hairs, waved hopelessly. I couldn't breathe for the horror of it—the thing looked like a grape.

Later on I described the moment to Pallas, who was dismissive. "Oh mom," she said, "Kiizhikok's much too intelligent to eat anything with legs that move."

Books. Why?

I've been to the islands and back. I've seen a great many books and held in my hands several that would be set behind glass in the rare books rooms of university libraries. I've touched the rock paintings, and read a fragment of their stories. Part of the trip is always the return, the way it shakes off you, the washing of duffel bags of clothes, the tons of catalogs that have collected in the mailbox. The next day, tick free, but sad over the tree and still disoriented, I walk over to our bookstore, Birchbark Books, in Minneapolis. I started it with my daughters for idealistic reasons—the native community, the neighborhood, the chance to work on something worthy with my girls. But really, in my deepest heart, I wonder now if I started it to cure myself of an affliction of books.

The door is blue because I love blue. It is an old door rescued from the knockdown of some haut-bourgeois Minneapolis house. It's beautiful. The window boxes, which I've planted with herbs and flowers, are overflowing now that it's August. And here is one of my favorite people in the world, Mr. Brian Baxter, who manages and oversees the getting and selling of the books at Birchbark Books! Brian, ah Brian, who will read "The Barrel-Organ" or maybe *Mean Soup* or maybe from *The Jungle Book* out loud and with perfect drama. Brian is also afflicted by books, but manages his addiction by having lived and sold books all of his life and by keeping only a small portion, several thousand, of the books that have passed through his hands.

Our store is pure comfort. Jelly beans, pretzels, and sour cherry bites are free. To create the store, we gutted a

dentist's office and brought unpeeled birch trees in to make a loft and birch boards to make floor-to-ceiling shelves. The store has good acoustics. We play our favorites in contemporary native music—from Black Lodge to Carlos Nakai's native flute, and of course Primeaux and Mike's peyote songs, perfect for reading and browsing. This bookstore looks like the inside of a cabin on Ober's island. There is an old Catholic confessional against one wall, bought from a salvage company. There are easy chairs that I've plucked from neighborhood alley dumpsters or boulevards, where they've been left for the taking. I've had them upholstered in soft denim. I was delighted to walk in one morning to find a writer I much admire sitting in one of these chairs and frowning at the corrections on a final proof of his new book. I am often thrilled when I can sit in the bookstore audience and listen to Susan Power or Jim Northrup read from their work. Writers sign our back wall. Our bathroom is papered with poems. Our office is the former dentist's closet where he prepared fillings and kept dank lunches in a stuttering two-foot refrigerator. Now the office/closet is loaded with books and book orders and too many bills to pay, for there is always that, the costliness of any great love.

There is sage, there is sweetgrass, there is red paint. This little bookstore is where I belong and where anyone can belong. It is a home for people who love books and a place that cannot be duplicated by any bookstore corporation—it is just too personal. It is an island, as lovingly itself as any in a lake. In our store, the greedy melancholy that Ober's books inspired falls away. It is an excellent and cheering thing to have a flow of books around you, to see them as they enter, and then take the money from people's hands as they disappear. They must be sold! Taken away! Still, besides my daily visits, sometimes I come to the store at night. I love to be among the books and to fuss them into pleasant order, just the way I love moving plants around in my garden. One of our booksellers, watching me, says, "Oh, you've come to love the books again?" Being around books is only half about actual reading, after all. The other part is talking about books with other people, a rich topic, and yet another is enjoying their presence. Sitting in the bookstore half-light I feel a great contentment.

Birchbark Books is just off Lake of the Isles. I didn't even think about this before I left, but that's it—the whole thing about islands and books. There really are two islands on Lake of the Isles and they are both wild islands, little places in the city where, from a canoe, I've seen great horned owls, black-crowned night-herons, arctic tern, dozens of black or painted turtles swirling off logs, and once a bald eagle. Maybe I live among the books and islands, and also must visit them in more remote places, because I've decided, in some deeply interior way unavailable to my conscious mind until I've started writing this book, that I will order my life to deal with a hoary old cliché.

This cliché has truly nagged at me. It is a question that I've asked myself periodically ever since I was nine years old. The question is: What book would you take to a desert island? I even have the question taped to the top of a cigar box on the bookstore counter, a request to customers to write their favorites on slips of paper, a way to find out about their tastes and discover titles that we've overlooked. What book would you take to a desert island—what a dismal thought! To have only one book to read over and over for years and years. Think of that miserable moment in the movie *Cast Away* when poor Tom Hanks opens a FedEx box and finds a *videocassette*. If only it had been a book! But which book should it have been? My solution is a dictionary. A dictionary would last and last. A dictionary would be a good thing

to have arrived in that FedEx box. But even better to be like
Oberholtzer and to store up 11,000. Or to be an Ojibwe
raised on stories and to contain many books in mind. Or
me, with a bookstore.

Books. Why?

AFTERWORD

Another Journey

The islands and the books still call us every summer. In June 2013 we set out in a newer version of the van—a 2005 Honda Odyssey, similarly packed to the gills. It is an innocuous silver gray, like most other cars. One of my daughters calls it the Manatee. I call it the Ark. Inside, there is my daughter Aza, the artist commissioned to make the cover of this book; Kiizh, who is now twelve; and me.

There is also Roadie, the travelin' dog, who was born the same year as Kiizh. Roadie has a maniacal devotion to my oldest daughter, Persia, but tolerates me. Roadie is recovering from surgery to her neck. A little white Jack Russell, she looks like a repaired stuffed animal with neat black stitches attaching her head to her busy muscular body. The other dog, Ryoga, has his own story. Named for the black pig of Aza's favorite childhood anime series, *Ranma ½*, this dog is a graceful wisp of charcoal. Roadie is outraged by his playful sorties. She glares in reproach from her tiny pink bed at the passenger's feet.

The many toys Kiizh had on the previous trip have been replaced by electronic devices—iPhone, laptop, iPad, and so on. After the forty-ninth parallel there's no reception, so I let her glut herself with screens for the first few hours. Anyway, we are visiting Persia on the way up north.

Ojibwemotadidaa

To my dear surprise, Persia has become the Ojibwe language leader in the family. For the past four years, she has been doing all she can to become fluent. This is her third summer as coordinator of an immersion Ojibwe language program held at the Fond du Lac Tribal and Community College. For three weeks in the summer and one weekend a month during the school year, absolutely no English is spoken there—cell phones and the abovementioned devices are confiscated upon entry. When I visited the program for a weekend last winter I excitedly opened my mouth to speak and found a well of nothingness. After two hours of stilted trying, I went to my room and fell into a dead sleep. My brain had saturated. That's how the whole weekend went. A few hours of Ojibwemowin, then a dead sleep as my brain cells absorbed conjugations. It is very difficult, people struggle, they cry. But they begin to speak. Persia loves her work.

She gets an evening off to check in with us, and, similarly, falls into a deep sleep in the motel room, clutching Roadie. We plot the rest of our travels. Next morning, we are off. First we go to Canada, but here things take an odd turn. While there we inadvertently, grudgingly, add a baby grackle to the ark.

Bineshiinh Island

This island in Lake of the Woods has innumerable bird-houses and is, like the predator-free zones in New Zealand, only for birds. There are no feral cats because the eagles get them. There are no squirrels because the vigilant owner and keeper of the island relocates them—to squirrel heaven. *Bineshiinh* means bird, and only birds are allowed.

Mergansers, mallards, buffleheads, arctic terns, goldfinches, purple finches, black and white warblers, warblers of many other varieties, rose-breasted and evening grosbeaks, ruby-throated hummingbirds, white-throated sparrows, grouse, blue jays, loons, and grackles.

Why books?

Why grackles?

It is here that we find a fledgling with a broken wing. Aza climbs a ladder and puts him back in the tree, close to his nest. We think the parents, who are still taking care of the other nestlings, might feed him. But although for an entire afternoon the baby grackle emits a hoarse *grack* as persistent and irritating as the low-battery signal on a smoke alarm, his parents swish around, ignoring him.

They have left him to die, Kiizh says.

Oh god, I think. Nature is harsh. But please don't let me rescue him, because the common grackle is a greedy, opportunistic, feckless, fearless, cold-eyed, only slightly glorified lizard of a bird.

And yet, what would Kiizh do?

Of course as the night comes on, the *grack* continues. I climb the ladder and scoop up the bird. We bring it in. I show the girls how to feed it. When the mouth opens, push a tiny gob of soft dog food down the gullet with the eraser end of a pencil. That's how I've saved crows. Drugged with protein, the nestling drops off. Next morning, this bird is focused. More food. Every few hours. We teach him to drink from a cup. His wing still drags, but he couldn't care less. He's growing right before our eyes! We daub an antibiotic cream on his wound. I contemplate getting him drunk on a few tablespoons of wine and sewing his wing together. I think my operation might kill him, but I also have a sense that not much can kill a grackle. He's a dystopic sort of bird—grackles will make it through climate change and every other sort of catastrophe humans throw at wildlife. So he gets his name.

Tenacious G

To get back down to Ober's Island, we now have to smuggle a grackle over the Canadian border. We put him in a cardboard grackle box, covered with a Costco bag. He has preempted Ryoga's seat. When hungry back there, he *grack*s. If he *grack*s at the border crossing, Kiizh plans to pretend to have lost her cell phone. But as I do at all border crossings now, I ask my daughter to take the wheel. No border guard ever troubles Aza, with her splendid eyes and radiant smile. We have the correct papers for the dogs and a bandanna around Roadie's neck, so nobody can see that her head is sewed on. The young guard gives us a cursory check and wishes Aza a good, a very good!, day, and we drive to Rainy River.

Island of the Book

We are meeting two friends who were married on this island last year. They have a granddaughter, Sequoia, nearly Kiizh's age. We don't travel lightly—but when Beth Waterhouse, executive director and wise woman of the island, shows up with a sturdy gear-toting vessel, she takes us in stride. She doesn't even raise an eyebrow at Tenacious.

From the first step onto the island, it is obvious that this place has made the right friends. Ten years have made it even better because of hardworking volunteers. The gardens are cheerful and immaculate—a huge bed of scarlet poppies is in full fancy-skirted bloom. Ober's house and the extraordinary fireplace that houses the spirit of a man named Charlie Friday, Giiwewosaadang, has been lovingly repaired. There is a fancy new Swedish bathroom with framed doggerel and a gate made of a swinging paddle. Each book in the collection has been catalogued, cleaned, repaired, and replaced where Ober left it. The scent of old paper and cedar fills the rooms of each house. The bookcases, some ingeniously hanging from rafters, have been invisibly reinforced.

The scale of the commitment to Ernest Oberholtzer's legacy, the intense thought that goes into each invisible improvement on his island, the forthright love, and the welcome. God! It is all so moving that my eyes tear up and I

put the grackle on my shoulder to remind me that the world
is hard. *Grack!* We are at home here. Aza chooses her spot
in the artist's cabin, close to the water, simple, with wooden
hooks for her clothing and dappled light. There, over the
coming week, she works and reworks the art piece that becomes the new cover of this book.

Asabikeshiinyag

The name in Ojibwe has to do with making nets, no surprise.
The surprise is how big they are, how suddenly they appear.
A wolf spider hunts in bounds across Aza's cream-colored
wall at night. The giant water spiders that bask on the rocks
near the bathing pools at Ober's are mottled like the stones,
and motionless. Aza nearly puts her hand on one. The most
amazing spider moment on the island occurs for me on the
loading dock, where I find six or more Halloweeny-looking
black, white, orange muscular fellows, a WWF-sized spider
gang, soaking up the heat. They don't like the vibrations of
my footsteps, and they stand on tiptoe. Swivel their faceted
eyes at me. I stop. They relax and start goofing around again.
One spider grabs another by the arm and slings his pal off
the dock into the water. Too much! I jump. They disappear.

We are here to work on the language, and Kiizh and
Sequoia decide to catalog and draw the spiders, turtles,
mosquitoes, deerflies, frogs, and fish that surround us, all in
Ojibwe. As they work on the pictures and words, I translate
the *Star Trek Book of Opposites*. My friend, the writer Gail
Caldwell, has a phrase in her book *New Life, No Instructions*.

Slower than the speed of light. That's my Ojibwe language learning. But I'm still at it, still trying. Same with our little independent whose picture I end with, Birchbark Books. The little store has not only survived but is beginning to float by itself. Mysterious. I am up north getting ready to go home, tend to the bookstore, and bring the grackle back down to be cured at the Wildlife Rehabilitation Center in St. Paul, when we hear about the tree.

Abiding

Of the great elm trees around my house described in the book, only one is left—the guardian of the west, Abiding Elm. The black locusts, Haywire and Entire Trust, have grown high enough to fill my third-story windows. There are hornbeam and white pines, a couple of maples to name, a catalpa that had its origins in my mother's flowerpot. I think a lot about the trees around my house.

Up north, my cell phone suddenly fills with calls. I talk with Persia and she tells me what happened, very tenderly, because she knows that this tree is special. Abiding was a boulevard elm planted by the city when my house was built. Abiding was felled with 3,500 trees in Minneapolis by the straight winds of a ferocious storm, following weeks of rain. These conditions toppled the trees with the biggest canopies, for with the soaking rains their roots lost purchase.

I try to be philosophical. It was an extremely beautiful elm of the classic wineglass shape. One by one the other elms succumbed to Dutch elm in spite of years of inoculation. Abiding stood alone, which made her more vulnerable. Fallen, she fills the backyard and makes it a jungle, impassable. With most of the power gone in Minneapolis, Persia has driven home from Fond Du Lac to an apocalyptic scenario, with people in line at the liquor store buying booze with cash and trees down everywhere, blocking streets. She makes it home only to find a camera crew at the smashed gate.

It is now four months since Abiding fell, and as I write this, the city is just now removing her 108-year-old stump. The crane claw worries, digs, worries, digs, and finally drags the stump out of the earth like a great tooth. Then I see why Abiding fell in the only place that would miss our house. Beneath the earth a mirror tree existed, the roots thick as the old branches, flowing toward the watery sand of the yard, away from the sterile dangers of the street.

Northern Lights

Lastly, this. Traditional Ojibwe people do not speak the names of those who have gone to the spirit world. Elders often shrug, hum, or look away when those names come into the conversation. After a generation, those names can be given to a close family member. That keeps the name alive. It is said that the person securely in the spirit world, visible dancing in the northern lights, is very happy to hear their name spoken by the living. But not using the names of the dead when referring to them, at least for some time, makes sense to me. It is a way of dealing with sorrow over the grievous loss of someone you love. I wasn't raised that way, but it makes sense.

It is not, as some say, because you are calling their spirit back. It is not, as some say, because the spirit might grow troubled and return. I think it is because not speaking the person's name keeps their spirit closer. It is somehow comforting not to speak of the person by name, but just to think of him leaping up rocks, scowling in his piercing way as he concentrates, smiling in delight or kindness, laughing in surprise, carrying his child on his shoulders. Mii'iw.

ACKNOWLEDGMENTS

To Ojibwe speakers and language experts—I tried my best to get it right and went over the book in 2002 with Tobasonakwutiban. He told me the words that describe shades of feeling. I spelled them as I heard them. The Ojibwe is a mixture of Canadian and Southern dialects. Any mistakes are mine. The names of plants are found in *Plants Used by the Great Lakes Ojibwa*, James E. Meeker, Joan E. Elias, John A. Heim. Published by Great Lakes Fish and Wildlife Commission. The words for "computer" and "rhinoceros" were given to me by Nawiigizisiban, Jim Clark. Again, I spelled them as I heard them, and included them because they are delightful. I would like to thank everyone mentioned in these pages. Miigwech.

ABOUT THE AUTHOR

LOUISE ERDRICH is a native of North Dakota, where she was raised by her Ojibwe-French mother and German-American father. She is the author of fourteen novels as well as volumes of poetry, short stories, children's books, and a memoir of early motherhood. Her novel *The Round House* won the National Book Award, and *The Plague of Doves* was a finalist for the Pulitzer Prize and won the Anisfield-Wolf Book Award. Her novel *Love Medicine* won the National Book Critics Circle Award. Louise Erdrich lives in Minnesota and is the owner of Birchbark Books, an independent bookstore.

ALSO BY **LOUISE ERDRICH**

FUTURE HOME OF THE LIVING GOD
A Novel
Available in Hardcover, Paperback, E-Book, Audio,
and Large Print

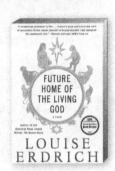

LAROSE
A Novel
Winner of the National Book Critics Circle Award
for Fiction
Available in Paperback, E-Book, Audio, and Large Print

THE ROUND HOUSE
A Novel
Winner of the National Book Award for Fiction
Available in Paperback, E-Book, Audio, and Large Print

THE PLAGUE OF DOVES
A Novel
Available in Paperback, E-Book, and Large Print

SHADOW TAG
A Novel
Available in Paperback and Large Print

THE PAINTED DRUM
A Novel
Available in Paperback, E-Book, and Large Print

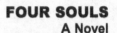

FOUR SOULS
A Novel
Available in Paperback and E-Book

THE MASTER BUTCHERS SINGING CLUB
A Novel
Available in Paperback and E-Book

THE LAST REPORT ON THE MIRACLES AT LITTLE NO HORSE
A Novel
Available in Paperback and E-Book

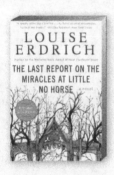

ANTELOPE WOMAN
A Novel
Available in Paperback and E-Book

TALES OF BURNING LOVE
A Novel
Available in Paperback

THE BINGO PALACE
A Novel
Available in Paperback

THE CROWN OF COLUMBUS
A Novel (co-written with Michael Dorris)
Available in Paperback

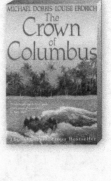

TRACKS
A Novel
Available in Paperback

THE BEET QUEEN
A Novel
Available in Paperback

LOVE MEDICINE
A Novel
Winner of the National Book Critics Circle Award in Fiction
Available in Paperback

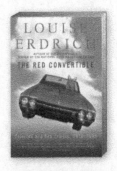

THE RED CONVERTIBLE
Selected and New Stories, 1978–2008
Available in Paperback and Large Print

ORIGINAL FIRE
Selected and New Poems
Available in Paperback and E-Book

THE BLUE JAY'S DANCE
A Memoir of Early Motherhood
Available in Paperback